THE HOME CHEF

COOKING WITH LOVE

By Helen Pope

Introduction

So the question from all my family and friends is ...... why did I write this cookbook? Well I once wrote a cook book for my lovely friend Julie. She was going through a bit of slump on the food front and bored with cooking so I thought I would make her my very own cook book for Christmas, using my favourite dishes to inspire her. It was just single pages of words printed onto coloured paper and stapled together. There were not even photographs of the recipes so I am not sure if it worked for her but I enjoyed doing it.

Since then I have dreamt of writing a proper cook book. If you know me you know I LOVE looking through cook books and currently have well over a hundred (closer to 200 probably but don't tell Andy!!). I do look through them pretty much every weekend, choosing what new recipes to make. It just takes me to my happy place and that cannot be a bad thing hey?

So the thought of having my name on the cover of my very own cook book will be a dream come true. I also thought it would be a great gift to give to Lauren and Adam to keep for the future so they can make recipes for their families continuing our family meals on to another generation. I just hope it turns out better than the stapled together effort I made for Julie all those years ago!

The original concept came up a long time ago during one of my long chatty walks with my brilliant dad. We were discussing the possibility of moving to Houston in America and by the time we finished the walk a plan had been hatched. I was going to move to Houston and once there write my own "English Recipes" Cook Book. I was going to start doing cooking courses from my home and set up an English style shop selling UK products such as Hellman's Mayonnaise and Heinz Tomato Sauce etc. Note that all the ingredients would be used in the cooking courses and in the book to help sales of the shop products. Not to mention selling the actual cook book. My Dad was born to be an entrepreneur – his mind just works that way and for anyone who knows my dad you will know what I mean!! We had built an entire wealthy empire in the time it took to walk 6 miles!

But once I arrived in Texas I realised that there is already heaps of expat foods in all the local supermarkets. I also realised that I didn't really have the nerve to actually host the cooking courses!! So I thought why not still give myself a challenge and make a cook book anyway. But instead of basing it around a cooking course I would just put in lots of recipes for all the really yummy stuff we like to eat at home as a family.

Although I am by no means a chef and can only just about call myself a home cook, I just enjoy doing it. I never use measurements and just add a bit here and a bit there, taste then add something else. Recipes were meant to be changed... no?? It has often happened that the family really enjoy a meal I have cooked and request it again but sadly by the time I come to make it I have forgotten what exactly I put in it – those meals became one hit wonders!!!!

Oh and on top of that I am not a photographer and I am rubbish at taking photos. Luckily for me I was given a few tips by my friend Wendy who happens to be an excellent photographer. However, quite a few of them are not the best but I decided I just wanted to roll with what I had as I thought it would keep it real. Some photographs may not look particularly great but they are definitely darn tasty so I hope you still give them a go.

Although I am not vegetarian or pescatarian, I do love eating vegetables and fish much more than meat on most occasions, so I have added lots of recipes to this book which can easily be changed to suit your mood or your eating preferences. All you have to do is just substitute the meat for veggies, pulses or even lentils. If you are a pescatarian change to veggies or fish. You can also spruce up the recipes by adding your own touches or leaving things out you don't like. As long as you make it your own and it is made with love then my job here is done!!

Time to say a quick thank you. Thank you Wendy for all your hours and hours and hours of help editing this book. Thanks for helping me with suggestions for the photos and your recommendations of how to make the book look the best it could be. I could never have done it without you so thank you from the bottom of my heart. Thanks to those that looked at shot after shot of photographs taken for the recipes, I know it was a bore. And thanks to those that gave me great advice on how to make this book actually happen.

Thanks also to Andrew and the kids for giving me so much support and encouragement and to poor Adam in particular who, being home alone with me, spent hours helping me take photographs, looking over ideas and coming up with suggestions for a million and one things. He was up and down the stairs after me shouting "ADAM!!!" more times than he cares to remember!! You are a STAR!!! And finally thanks to EVERYONE who listened to me talking about it endlessly for months and months on end. I will bet you are glad that it is finally finished!! Everyone of you helped me make this dream come true and you all mean the world to me.

Top Tips

Top tips you that will change the way you cook, save time and make your life a whole lot easier. In some cases it will also save on your wallet!

Buy a Slow Cooker

If you haven't got one already – BUY ONE!! I love mine and I use it ALL the time. It is so easy to just throw food in and leave it to cook while you get on with other things. After 2-4 hours it is done and ready to serve and all you have to wash up is the inside cooking pot. I invested in a 3 function Crockpot which sautés the food in the pot first before you slow cook so no need for extra pans etc. It also has a pressure cook settings for meats, poultry, beans and soups which quickens cooking times. On top of that if you are not home when it finishes cooking it sits there for up to 4 hours just keeping food warm. I would be lost without mine.

Keep herbs fresh for longer

My tip for keeping herbs longer is to put them in an air tight container with a piece of kitchen roll underneath and on top of them. Or wrap them in kitchen roll inside a sealed bag where no air can get in - it works for me!! I also use this technique for my peeled garlic. They last for months.

Breading food

I have always watched on TV that to bread something you need to roll in flour, dip into egg and then dip it into breadcrumbs. This can take a while to prepare and is messy. I came across this easier method years ago and I have never used any other technique since. I have even converted my Mum!!

It is a simple as rubbing a very thin layer of mayonnaise (it has eggs in and acts as a sticking agent) over your protein or vegetable and then dip into a plate of breadcrumbs and squish down. It can then either be fried or baked in the oven depending on preference. I promise you it sounds pretty odd but as long as you are not too heavy handed with the mayo you won't even taste it. Honestly it was a game changer for me.

Making a cheats White Sauce

Making a white sauce can take a little time and I often end up with lumps in it as I always try and add the milk too quickly. Even when I try and be good by adding the milk in slowly I still often ended up with those pesky flour lumps.

Cheats way - simply add the cold milk, margarine (or butter) and the flour to a pan and heat stirring all the time as you go. Keep stirring until you have a thick sauce like consistency. Once it is ready you could add cheese to make a cheese sauce for cauliflower cheese or the layers for a lasagne. Thanks Auntie Pauline!!

Top Tips

Cooking Rice

This is a lot of people nemesis but I have come up with a fool proof way to ensure that your rice doesn't get all gloopy and stick together. It will come out light and fluffy every time. I like to use basmati rice as I just feels it holds its shape better. The first tip is to make sure that you rinse the rice before cooking. I do this at least three times until the water no longer goes cloudy. The second tip is to add double parts water to single part rice. So 1 mug of rice will need 2 mugs of water. The last tip is to add the rice and water to a pan and bring to the boil. Then leave for a couple of minutes before turning off the heat and putting a lid on it. Leave for 15-20 minutes or until all the water has been absorbed. Then simply use a fork to fluff up the rice.

Prawns

When cooking with raw prawns make sure that you remove the intestine artery (known as deveining) before cooking. To do this simply use a sharp knife to cut along the black vein on the back of the prawn and remove. The artery will not harm you if you did eat it but it can be quite gritty so it doesn't taste so good!!!

Stains in cups and mugs

Fed up with tea and coffee stains inside your cups and mugs. Quick tip, thanks to my Mum in Law, sprinkle in some salt and scrunch around with the sponge scrubber. The abrasion will help remove the stains so quickly you won't believe your eyes!

Burnt Pans

Ever left a pan bubbling away only to forget about it and by the time you realise your food is burnt to a crisp? I know I have done it many a time – too many times to be honest. So another Mother in Law tip – add some distilled white vinegar and a splash of water and bring it to the boil. Leave for about 10 minutes bubbling away and then wash with soapy water. It will really reduce your scrubbing time. But on the negative side your house smells for hours afterwards – especially if you don't like vinegar which my boys do not!!

Top Tips

Freezing

Whenever I make rice, pasta or mashed potato I ALWAYS make too much – I just can't ever seem to judge it right. But once it is cool any leftovers can be put in a small plastic bag or pot and frozen until you need it for another meal. When ready to eat defrost the portions first then reheat.

For the rice just poke a hole in the bag to stop it exploding then microwave until piping hot. The Pasta can be reheated super quickly by just putting into a colander then pouring boiling water over it. The mash might look a bit runny when defrosted but once you re heat it in the microwave until piping hot and stir it up it will go back to the original consistency.

Food goes out of date quicker than we think and is sadly often wasted. I hate waste and I freeze EVERYTHING!! If anything is about to go out of date it goes into the freezer. If anything is left over from dinner, no matter how small, it goes into the freezer. When making family meals I often make too much on purpose so I can freeze a portion or two for a later date. I am the freezer queen.

Apart from leftover meals there are so many things you can freeze which you might not have thought of. Here are just a few:

Chillies, nuts, herbs, ginger, pizza and bread dough, bread, cooked chicken, or sandwich meats.

Cheese freezes brilliantly. You can add blocks or grated cheese. You can even take it out and let it defrost, use what you need and stick back in the freezer.

Lots of vegetables (best chopped up) such as leeks, onions, celery, peppers or carrots freeze well but can be a bit mushy once defrosted so these work well going into recipes that require them to be cooked. Mashed carrot & parsnip freezes really well and can just be microwaved to reheat when serving.

Blueberries, blackberries, raspberries and strawberries (hull them first). Bananas also freeze however they become soft and gloopy once defrosted so would work well in a smoothie or in a banana loaf or muffins.

If you have any wine left at the end of a bottle try adding it to an ice cube tray and freezing. They can then be popped out and added to dishes that need wine without opening a whole bottle. Just for the record I never have to do this as I never have any wine left at the end of my bottle!!

A last freezer tip is to write a date and contents on whatever you freeze so you know what is and when it was put in the freezer. I always move things around so the oldest things are on the top of the freezer compartment so they get used up first and do not end up getting left at the bottom and going out of date in the freezer as well! It also helps to know what you are taking out. I have in the past been known to defrost something for dinner only to realise it wasn't what I thought it was. That can hamper dinner plans I can tell you!!

My Store Cupboard Essentials

Oils

Olive oil (good for dressings)
Vegetable oil (good for frying or baking)
Toasted sesame oil (good for flavouring, especially for Asian cooking but use sparingly)

Vinegars

Mainly I use white and red wine vinegar but I also like to use apple cider and balsamic. I use rice wine vinegar a lot too.
Malt vinegar is an essential for me and Lauren for chips but the boys both go "yuk"!!!

Condiments and Sauces

Mayonnaise, Salad Cream
Salad Dressings
Tomato Puree
Honey
Ketchup
Mustard (Wholegrain, Dijon and American Yellow)
Sauces (Soy, Hoisin, Fish, Teriyaki, Worcestershire, Chilli)
All types of hot sauce

My Spice Rack

Oregano, Italian seasoning, thyme, sage, basil, bay leaves
Cumin and coriander (whole and ground), chilli powder, turmeric, fennel seeds, mustard seeds, cardamom seeds, Sesame seeds, cayenne pepper, red chili flakes, paprika, garlic salt, coarse black pepper, sea salt

Canned Goods

Canned tuna (a must in our house and used sooo often)
Chicken stock/broth
Chopped tomatoes (if I have less than 2 tins available at any time I get totally stressed)
Beans (we use heaps of beans – cannellini, red kidney beans and of course Baked Beans!!)

Pasta, Rice, Legumes

Pasta (every type of pasta you can think of - spaghetti, penne, macaroni, lasagne ... the list goes on. Adam would eat pasta every day of the week if we let him so we buy lots!!)
Basmati rice (I love that it cooks so well without going "gloopy")
Risotto rice (Adam loves risotto nearly as much as pasta so we use lots of this too)
Green and red dried lentils
Couscous, Rice Noodles

Fresh Produce

Salad (I always have a stash of lettuce, tomatoes and spring onions as a bare minimum)

Onions and garlic (I put onions and garlic in EVERYTHING!! Even if it's not in the recipe!! I even buy the garlic ready peeled. Try it … once you have you will never go back to peeling it yourself!!)

Vegetables (I always have a stocked fridge with vegetables like broccoli, carrots, cauliflower, peppers and celery)

Fruit (mangoes, tangerines, strawberries, blueberries and grapes mostly)

Fresh ginger

Lemons and limes (I use heaps)

Cheese (parmesan and cheddar mostly)

Herbs (I always have coriander in. It is a love/hate herb but for me it's a LOVE!! I also love fresh basil but I must admit as I am not green fingered it never lasts very long!)

Freezer Food

Frozen peas

Frozen sweetcorn

Cooked chicken portions

Go to staples (chicken, pork chops, steak, salmon, tilapia fillets, and prawns)

Mince (I always have a portion of beef, turkey and pork mince available)

Chips (Just for when my Dad comes around to dinner)

Bread (keeps longer and you can just leave it to defrost when you need it or throw it in the toaster)

Ice-Cream (for Adam!!)

Other

Stock Cubes (beef, chicken and vegetable)

Gravy granules. We use them to thicken the mince in my Shepherd's Pie recipe. Or occasionally to make a quick chips, cheese and gravy (well for me and Lauren anyways – a "NO GO" from the boys though!!)

Flour, all purpose and bread

Sugar, granulated and brown

Breadcrumbs, Italian flavoured and panko

Mixed nuts

Capers

Olives

Conversion Table

UK

Stock Cube
Stock Cube with water
Coriander
Tomato Puree
Beef/Pork Mince
Beef/Pork Fillet
Prawns
Runner Bean/Green Bean
Aubergine
Courgette
Turnip/Swede
Spring Onions
Rocket
Double Cream
Chopped Tomatoes
Flaked Sea Salt
Extra Virgin Olive Oil
Chips
Crisps
Biscuits
Grill
Cling Film

Approximately
236ml
140g
225g
200g

USA

Bouillon
Broth
Cilantro
Tomato Paste
Ground Beef/Pork
Beef/Pork Tenderloin
Shrimp
String Bean
Egg Plant
Zucchini
Rutabaga
Green Onions/Scallions
Arugula
Heavy Whipping Cream
Crushed Tomatoes
Kosher Salt
EVOO
Fries
Potato Chips
Cookies
Broil
Plastic Wrap

1 Cup of
Liquid
Flour
Butter/Fat
Sugar

Section   Page

Starters/Salads

I love a salad but they are often quite boring and sometimes weighed down with heavy dressings so not as healthy as you would like. I love to find a salad that is full of flavour and excites me when I am eating it. All the recipes can be adapted and are great for light lunches, starters or even side portions to a main meal.

Soups

Andrew used to take soup to work almost every day so I would spend a weekend making lots of different batches of soup to be individually portioned out and frozen. The night before work I would choose a soup and take it out to defrost ready for the next day. It was a different soup every day. Choices like pea & ham, spicy bean & taco, Mexican chicken, bacon & lentil, broccoli & parmesan, roasted tomato, leek & potato or roasted squash, chilli and lime. I have chosen just a few here which are my favourites and easiest to make.

Seafood

I love fish. Any type really. I try and eat it at least once a week but normally ends up two or three times. Often I will make some red meat recipe for the boys and fish for me. People are often scared of cooking fish but don't be. The recipes I have added here are super easy and super tasty. Not to mention relatively quick to cook and healthy to eat.

Pork and Poultry

I am not that keen on pork so you will notice not too many recipes here but I do quite like a pork tenderloin and I can tell you Andy makes the most AMAZING pork Sunday roast. The gravy is just to die for and his Yorkshire puddings are a real treat. But chicken is one of the things I probably use the most of. It is reasonably priced, easy to cook with and there are so many available and different recipes to choose from which is why I found it so difficult to decide which ones to pick for this book. But I have chosen just a handful of my favourite recipes here.

Meat

I try to keep eating red meat down to once a week for the family but sometimes this goes a bit by the wayside as the boys do like it. Most recipes I have chosen are Andrew and the kid's favourites like shepherd's pie and chilli con carne. But I can't lie I am a bit partial to my lasagne and meatballs are one of my favourites too.

Section	Page

Curries

There isn't a section on curries but you will find quite a few in this book. I could write a whole book on curries alone (my next mission??). They are one of my favourite things to eat. If you haven't cooked many curries from scratch then the list of ingredients may sound a bit daunting on some of the recipes but once you have bought them, made the curry and realised how tasty and easy they are to make you will be pleased you took the plunge. For me there is absolutely no comparison between home-made v a jar (in my opinion anyway!!).

Vegetarian

I mostly try my best to be as healthy as possible with my meals. When I portion up I normally have a smallish protein, small carbs and a ton of vegetables. Not because I am trying to lose weight but because I LOVE vegetables. I also try and have at least one night a week where I only eat a vegetarian meal, much to the disgust of the boys ha ha!! I hope you enjoy the vegetarian sides and mains. Yum Yum Veggies bum!!

Sweet Treats

Just to let you know, I DO NOT have a sweet tooth. Savoury over sweet every time for me. And for that reason I think I just don't enjoy making deserts and cakes and in turn means I am not very good at them. For example, one year for Laurens birthday I decided to make her a birthday cake and to try and make sure it didn't go wrong I made a pre-bought, boxed one. It still went wrong and all the guests had to eat the cake with a spoon from a paper cup. I have had frozen torts Andy has had to drill through to cut up, cheesecakes not set and fondant cakes rock solid with absolutely no sign of any goo!!! The list goes on and on. That is why this section is the smallest of the book. But as this IS a cookbook I managed to team up with Adam (who loves to cook them) and found a few fool proof recipes just to show willing. You will notice a common theme though – CHOCOLATE!!

Super Easy Salad Dressings

Blue Cheese (great with a cobb salad or even just as a dip for veggies)

Mix together 1-2 tbsp of crumbled blue cheese, 1 tbsp mayonnaise, 2 tbsp plain unsweetened yoghurt, 1 tsp lemon juice, 1-2 tbsp water, enough to loosen.

Caesar (toss with a salad leaf like romaine and add croutons if you like)

Mix together 3 tbsp of mayonnaise, 1 tsp Dijon mustard, 1 tsp Worcestershire sauce, 1 crushed garlic clove, 1 tsp anchovy paste, 1 tbsp parmesan cheese, pinch of salt and pepper and about 1 tbsp lemon juice (add more if required).

Super Easy Vinaigrettes

Lemon and Mustard (great over salads or cooked vegetables)

Whisk together 1 ½ cups of lemon juice, 1 tbsp olive oil, 1 ½ tbsp Dijon mustard and a pinch of salt and pepper.

Balsamic (great over cooked broccoli or carrots)

Whisk together 1 ½ tbsp of balsamic vinegar, 1 tsp olive oil, ½ tsp Dijon mustard, 1 crushed garlic clove and a squeeze of lemon juice.

Super Easy Tomato Sauce

To make a super speedy tomato sauce instead of the one shown in my meatball recipe why not try this?

Heat the oven to 400°F / 200 °C / Gas Mark 6

Now simply add a tin of chopped tomatoes to a casserole dish along with some crushed garlic, oregano, dried basil, Italian herbs, a pinch of salt and pepper and a really good glug of red wine.

Put in the oven for 30 minutes to let the red wine cook off and the flavours combine. Then take it out and add some fresh torn basil leaves. Return to the oven for a further 15 minutes or until you have a thick sauce. You can also add chilli flakes for extra heat if you fancy.

Super Easy Marinades

All the marinades below work well with either fish, meat, poultry, pork or even vegetables but I have highlighted what has worked best for me in the past.

Spice Master (works really well with salmon and seabass)

Add 2 tsp of each, coriander seeds, cumin seeds and fennel seeds to a dry pan and roast gently for a few minutes until you start to smell the fragrance of the seeds. Be careful not to burn them. Take off the heat and add in 2 tbsp of lemon juice, 1 tsp garlic powder, 2 tsp paprika and a sprinkle of salt. Mix together to form a paste. If it is too dry just add a small splash of water. Marinade for a few hours if you have time.

Green Thai (works really well with chicken and great for a BBQ)

Roughly chop 3 garlic cloves, 1 thumb sized piece of peeled ginger, 2 spring onions, 2 lemongrass stalks (use the inside soft white part only), 5 lime leaves (this gives it such a unique flavour) and then add to a food processor. Pour in 1 tbsp fish sauce, 1 tsp olive oil and blend. If it needs more liquid just add a touch of water until you have a sauce like consistency. You will have a vibrant green sauce. Marinade overnight if possible but if not able just as long as you can.

Green India (works especially well with white fish as it soaks up the flavour)

Put ¼ white onion, ½ cinnamon stick, ½ green chilli, 1 tsp de-podded cardamom seeds, ¼ tsp black peppercorns, 1 garlic clove, 5g fresh coriander (a big handful stalks and all), ½ juice of a lime (about 1 tbsp) and a pinch of salt into a food processor. Blitz together to form a sauce then marinade for about 30 minutes. If using fish do not leave longer than 30 minutes as the lime juice will start to cook it. Try using seabass, tilapia or cod.

Lemongrass (works great with chicken especially thighs)

To a bowl add 2 tbsp of lemon juice, 2 tbsp finely chopped lemongrass (use the inside soft white part only), ½ tbsp brown sugar, 1 tbsp crushed garlic, 2 tsp fish sauce and 1 tbsp soy sauce. Give it a mix then marinade overnight if possible but if not able just as long as you can.

Five Spice and Lemon (works great with chicken thighs or drums)

Mix together 3 tbsp of brown sugar, a thumb sized piece of grated ginger, juice of 2 lemons, 2 crushed garlic cloves, 5 tbsp soy sauce, 1 tsp Chinese five-spice, and 1 tbsp white wine. Give it a mix then marinade overnight if possible but if not able just as long as you can.

500g Strong Bread Flour
325 ml tepid Water
7g Dried Yeast
A glug of Olive Oil
Pinch of Salt
Toppings of choice depending
on what you fancy

NOTE
There are lots of topping options for
this bread. Try poking in some halved
cherry tomatoes and basil, some feta
and tomato, rosemary and olives, blue
cheese and thyme or anything at all
that takes your fancy. You could also
just leave it plain with a sprinkle of sea
salt and it will be just as nice.

*Try this with a dipping sauce of olive oil
and balsamic vinegar mixed together or
alongside something like oven roasted
goats cheese topped with cherry tomatoes.
It would work really well as part of a
charcuterie board or why not serve it
simply with hummus or any type of dip.*

Focaccia Bread

This Focaccia Bread is relatively easy to prepare, it is just the
proving times which tends to be a little bit lengthy but it is so
worth it. Great dinner party table piece.

INSTRUCTIONS

Heat Oven to 400°F / 200 °C / Gas Mark 6

In a bowl mix together the tepid water and the yeast. Add the flour and a
glug of olive oil and stir with a fork until you have a dough like consistency.
Flour your work surface and your hands and knead the dough for around 10
minutes or until stretchy. Place your empty bowl over the dough and leave
to prove for around 45 minutes.

Lightly oil a cooking tray and stretch your dough out evenly on it. Sprinkle
another small glug of olive oil and again spread out evenly making small
welts using your thumb as you go. Push down your topping of choice into
the dough then cover with a damp, warm tea towel and leave to prove for
another 45 minutes.

Once the dough has doubled in size, sprinkle with a pinch of salt and bake
for 20-25 minutes until cooked. Leave to cool for around 10 minutes before
serving.

INGREDIENTS

2lb Carrots
Splash of Olive Oil
1 Onion, finely chopped
2 Garlic Cloves, crushed
1 tsp Sugar
1 Green Chilli, finely chopped
2 Spring Onions, finely chopped
1 tsp of each Coriander and Cumin
1 tsp Paprika
½ tsp of each Ginger and Cinnamon
1 tbsp White Wine Vinegar
Squeeze of Lemon Juice
Large handful of fresh Coriander
Leaves, finely chopped
Pinch of Salt and Pepper

You can serve this salad hot or cold. It can be eaten on its own for a super light lunch or you could serve it alongside a fish dish or even pork or poultry for an evening meal.

Spicy Carrot Salad

Serves 4

I love salad full stop. I eat it all the time but sometimes it does get a little boring. But there is nothing boring about this salad. It does take a little time to prepare but it is full of intense flavours and it is really delicious.

INSTRUCTIONS

Peel the carrots and cut into matchsticks approximately 5 centimetres long. Try to cut them to roughly the same size so they cook evenly. Then either steam in the microwave for 2 minutes (until tender but still with a crunch) or boil in a saucepan for about 5 minutes then drain.

While the carrots are cooking add the olive oil and onions to a pan and sauté for approximately 10 minutes on a medium heat until they are soft and just starting to brown. Now add the garlic and cook for another minute.

Add in the cooked carrots along with all the remaining ingredients (except the coriander) and stir for a few more minutes until well combined. Take off the heat, add in the fresh coriander and stir again. If needed add more salt, pepper or lemon juice depending on your personal taste.

INGREDIENTS

4 Chicken Breasts or Thighs, cooked
1 Orange, zested and juiced
2 tsp of Dijon Mustard
2 tsp Wholegrain Mustard
1 tbsp Honey
2 small bulbs of Fennel
4 tbsp fresh Herbs
(try Tarragon, Dill, Coriander,
Basil or a mixture)
Pinch of Salt and Pepper

This is a really tasty lunch option but you can easily uplift it to an evening meal by serving the chicken alongside the fennel salad (instead of inside it) and adding some new potatoes or a baked potato. Why not have a French Baguette on the side too!

Chicken and Fennel Salad

Serves 4

This is a great lunch option when you don't want a basic salad. The flavours of the fennel, honey and orange just work. Plus it takes absolutely no time at all to make.

INSTRUCTIONS

In a bowl whisk together the orange zest, orange juice, Dijon mustard, Wholegrain mustard and the honey until well combined.

Chop the cooked chicken into bite sized pieces and set aside. Then chop the fennel into thin slices so it resembles a coleslaw type mixture and also set aside. Roughly chop your herbs of choice.

Add the chicken and fennel to the bowl of dressing along with your herbs of choice and mix everything together. Give it a taste then adjust the seasoning with salt and pepper if required. You are now ready to serve!

INGREDIENTS

32 large Raw Prawns
(Peeled and de-veined)
1 tbsp Olive Oil
4 tsp Chilli Powder
2 tsp Cumin
2 Garlic Cloves, crushed
Pinch of Salt and Pepper
1 large Mango
1 Lemon, halved
A handful of Coriander, chopped

You could also serve this as a salsa type dish by cooking as per above but chopping the mango and prawns into cubes, mixing together and maybe adding in some chopped spring onions. Try serving it alongside a fish fillet such as seabass, cod or a salmon fillet would work well too.

Chilli Prawns with Mango

Serves 4

This is a really good alternative if you are trying to avoid fatty foods (it is super tasty if you are not too!!). It would be a great starter for a curry night or just a light lunch.

INSTRUCTIONS

In a frying pan (big enough to fit the prawns in a single layer) mix together the olive oil, chilli powder, cumin, garlic and the salt and pepper. Add in the prawns and mix them around until they are fully coated with the sauce. Leave to marinade for about an hour.

Once ready to serve peel and cut the mango into slices and place equal portions onto 4 plates. Fry the prawns in the frying pan they were marinated in until they have turned pink and are cooked through. This should only take 1 to 2 minutes on each side. Be careful not to overcook them as they will become dry and chewy.

Add the prawns to the plates and squeeze the lemon juice over both the prawns and the mango. Finish off by sprinkling the chopped coriander over the top. Serve and enjoy.

INGREDIENTS

16 large Raw Prawns, peeled
½ tsp Cumin Seeds
½ tsp Coriander Seeds
½ tsp Chilli Flakes
Pinch of Salt and Pepper
½ tsp Honey
Juice of a Lime (approximately 2 tbsp)
1 tsp Fish Sauce
Handful of Fresh Coriander, chopped
½ Bag of ready-made Coleslaw Mix
Splash of Olive Oil

You could serve this salad alongside a portion of crusty bread and butter if you want a more substantial lunch. Or why not even stuff it into a baguette or pitta. Whichever way you serve it I think you might be making it again!

Zingy Prawn Salad

Serves 2

This is a light and healthy salad option which packs a huge flavour punch. Just don't forget to de-vein the prawns.

INSTRUCTIONS

In a small pan heat the cumin and coriander seeds for a few minutes or until you start to smell the aromatics. Place into a pestle and mortar and crush. Transfer to a bowl and add the chilli flakes, salt and pepper and mix. Add the prawns and coat well then leave to marinade for about 15 minutes.

While the prawns are marinating make your dressing by whisking together the honey, lime juice, fish sauce and the coriander in a bowl. Taste and adjust the seasoning as required. Add in the coleslaw mix and give it a good stir. I like to scrunch it up using my hands to let all the flavours marry together nicely.

Now fry your prawns in a splash of olive oil for just a minute or two on each side or until pink and fully cooked. Make sure you do not overcook the prawns. Then simply place the coleslaw mix on a plate and top with the cooked prawns. You could also serve this by just cutting the prawns in half then stirring them into the coleslaw mix so you get an even bite of everything in each mouthful.

INGREDIENTS

2 Limes, juiced and zested
1 thumb sized piece of Ginger, grated
2 tbsp Honey
2 tbsp Soy Sauce
4 Spring Onions
4 tbsp fresh Coriander, chopped
Splash of Sesame Oil
Pinch of Chilli Flakes (optional)
300g bag of ready-made Coleslaw Mix
4 Chicken Breasts, cooked
2 Peaches, cut into small cubes

You could switch out the chicken for prawns here and that would work really well too. Fried Tofu in replacement of the chicken would be a great vegetarian option. Or just leave the chicken out all together and serve it as an Asian Coleslaw next to some grilled meat.

Chicken and Peach Salad

Serves 4

This salad most definitely has an oriental feel about it. The peaches and chicken combination work really well with the tanginess of the dressing. You could replace the coleslaw mix with something like rocket or watercress. Why not try adding some chopped peanuts over the top at the end to give it a nice crunch.

INSTRUCTIONS

In a bowl mix together the lime juice, lime zest, ginger, honey, soy sauce, spring onions, coriander, sesame oil and chilli flakes (if using).

Taste and adjust the flavour if you think it needs a little more lime juice, honey or soy for instance.

Shred the chicken into bite sized pieces then add that to the bowl along with the coleslaw mix and peaches. Give it a stir and it is ready!!

How quick was that?!

Soups

All Recipes Serve 4 with possibly left overs depending on appetites!

These soups all freeze really well so I often make a big batch by doubling the recipe and putting the leftovers into individual freezer containers for lunch at a later date. To each recipe add additional stock or water as you go if it gets too thick and as much salt and pepper as you like depending on your preferences and taste.

INGREDIENTS

Splash of Olive Oil
4 skinless Chicken Thighs
1 Onion, finely chopped
1 Red Pepper, cubed
4 Garlic Cloves, finely chopped
1 tbsp of Tomato Puree
400g tin of Chopped Tomatoes
1 pint Chicken Stock
1 tbsp of both Cumin and Coriander
½ Red Chilli, finely chopped (add more or less depending how hot you like it)
1 tbsp of Chipotle Paste (or from a tin, finely chopped)
A handful of fresh Coriander, chopped
Juice of a Lime to finish

Mexican Chicken Soup

I love this soup because it is super yummy, super easy and super healthy. It can be slow cooked on the hob or in a slow cooker, either works well. You can also power up on protein by adding beans such as cannellini to bulk out the soup.

INSTRUCTIONS

Add the oil to a pan and sauté the onions and red pepper for around 10 minutes or until softened. Add the garlic and cook for a further 2 minutes. Add the tomato puree and cook for a another minute.

Now add all the remaining ingredients (except the coriander and lime juice) and give it a good stir and bring to the boil.

Once boiling turn down the heat to low, put the pan lid on and simmer very gently for at least one hour or until the chicken starts to fall off the bone. If using a slow cooker set it to 4 hours and leave.

Once the chicken is tender take it out of the soup and leave to cool slightly until you are able to handle with your hands. Then remove all the bones and shred the chicken into small pieces.

Pop the chicken back in the pan and mix. Add in the coriander and lime juice.

Depending on your taste feel free to add more lime juice if you think it needs it – I usually do!!. Garnish with additional coriander (if you like coriander ...... I LOVE IT!!!).

INGREDIENTS

Splash of Olive Oil
1 Onion, finely chopped
2 Garlic Cloves, finely chopped
4 medium Tomatoes, finely chopped
4 tbsp Bacon Bits or small pack
of Pancetta (fried)
1 pint Chicken Stock
1 tbsp Oregano
300g of Red Split Lentils

Bacon and Lentil Soup

This soup would warm your cockles on a winter's day (and any other day for that matter). It is also really good for you as the lentils are high in protein and other essential minerals and vitamins.

INSTRUCTIONS

Cover the lentils with water and bring them to the boil. Once boiling turn down to a simmer and leave to cook until tender and "mushy". While cooking discard any scum that accumulates on the top of the cooking water. Add extra water as you go along if the lentils become too dry before they finish cooking.

Meanwhile add the oil and onions to a pan and sauté until the onions start to soften. Add the garlic and fry for a few more minutes. Now add the chopped tomatoes and cook until the tomatoes become mushy and broken down. At this point add the chicken stock, bacon bits (or pancetta) and the oregano and simmer for about 10-15 minutes or until the onions have completely cooked and are soft.

Once the onion and tomato mixture and the lentils are ready just combine both pans together and stir well to mix.

INGREDIENTS

1 Onion, finely chopped
2 Garlic Cloves, finely chopped
1 large head of Broccoli
4 medium sized Potatoes, peeled
and cubed
1 pint Chicken Stock
The rinds of 2 small parmesan blocks
(or 4 tbsp Parmesan Cheese, grated)
1 tsp Thyme

Broccoli and Parmesan Soup

This soup takes no time at all to make as everything is just thrown in and yet it still tastes scrummy. You could substitute the parmesan for something like a stilton to give it more of a punch or you could leave out the cheese all together.

INSTRUCTIONS

Just add all the ingredients to a pan, bring it to a boil then reduce down to a simmer and cover with a lid. Cook for approximately 20 minutes or until the onions, potatoes and broccoli are soft and falling apart.

Take out the parmesan rind (if using) then mash the soup up with a potato masher. You could blitz the soup in a food blender for a finer consistency but I prefer the rustic taste and texture when it is just mashed.

INGREDIENTS

For the Thai Curry Base

2 Garlic Cloves
1 thumb sized piece of Ginger
I tsp Chilli Powder
1 tsp Cinnamon
1 tbsp Coriander
1 tsp Turmeric
1 Red Onion, quartered
Pinch of Salt
400ml tin Light Coconut Milk
400ml tin Chicken Stock (or stock
cube and water)

For the Green Sauce

Large handful of fresh Coriander Stalks
1 Jalapeno Chilli (add more or less
depending on heat preference)
2 Garlic Cloves
Zest and juice of 1 Lime

Veg Option – Make it vegetarian by
adding sweet potatoes, butternut squash
or pretty much any vegetable. Cooking
times will change depending on what
vegetables you use.

*You can add any protein to this dish.
Chicken takes the longest to cook whereas
prawns take no time at all.
You could also add meat but I would only
use fillet steak cut into thin strips which
also takes only minutes to cook.*

Tasty Thai Curry

Serves 4

The kids are not huge curry fans but as this recipe is sooooo
delicious I still make it for 4 people and freeze half ready for
next time. Winner, winner Thai Curry dinner!

INSTRUCTIONS

Start by adding all the ingredients in the Thai Curry Base (except the
coconut milk and chicken stock) to a food processor and blitz into a puree.
Add the puree to your pan and cook on a medium heat for approximately 5
minutes.

Add the coconut milk and chicken stock to the pan and bring to the boil.
Now reduce to a simmer and cook uncovered for 10-15 minutes.

While the base is cooking add all the ingredients in the Green Sauce to a
food processor and blitz to a puree. Add a splash of water if needed.

Once the base is cooked add your protein or/and vegetables and cook for a
further 5-10 minutes or until cooked through. Mix in the green sauce. Taste
and add additional lime juice if needed. Serve over rice.

INGREDIENTS

4 Salmon Fillets
4 Egg Noodle Nests
8 oz tin of Chopped Pineapples
1 thumb sized piece Ginger, grated
2 tbsp Hoisin Sauce
2 tbsp Rice Wine Vinegar
2 tbsp Soy Sauce
2 tbsp Teriyaki Sauce
1 Red Chilli, chopped (add more or less
depending on heat preference)
Juice of 1 - 2 Limes
Handful of fresh Coriander, chopped
Handful of Peanuts, chopped
2 Spring Onions, chopped
1 tbsp Sesame Seeds (optional)

Alternatively you could serve the salmon on rice with the pineapple salsa drizzled over the top. This recipe would also work really well with prawns. Just add the prawns to the noodles when you add the salsa and cook until the prawns have turned pink.

Salmon with Noodles and Pineapple Salsa

Serves 4

Looking for a Chinese take-away but want to save some money and eat a little healthier? If yes then this is your go to recipe. As with some Indian dishes there are quite a few store bought ingredients but once you have them in your cupboard and you have tried this dish you will want to make this recipe again and again.

INSTRUCTIONS

Heat Oven to 400°F / 200 °C / Gas Mark 6

Sprinkle the salmon with your seasoning of choice (salt and pepper, paprika or any seasoning that comes to hand) then wrap in tin foil and bake in the oven until just cooked, approximately 10 minutes depending on size.

Meanwhile make a salsa by finely chopping the pineapple and adding to a bowl along with all of the juice. Mix in the grated ginger, hoisin sauce, rice wine vinegar, soy sauce, teriyaki sauce, red chilli, lime juice and the coriander.

Cook the noodles as per the instructions then toss with the pineapple salsa mixture. Return to the pan and reheat for a further minute. Taste and add more lime juice or soy sauce if needed. Serve the noodles topped with the cooked salmon. To finish off sprinkle over sesame seeds, chopped peanuts, spring onions and additional coriander if you like!

INGREDIENTS

4 Salmon Fillets
1 heaped tbsp Cumin Seeds
1 heaped tbsp Coriander Seeds
1 tsp Sesame Oil
1 tbsp Fish Sauce
1 tbsp Chilli Sauce (add more or less depending on heat preference)
Juice of 1 Lime
2 tbsp Honey
2 tbsp Water
Bag of Rocket
8 pieces of Sun-Dried Tomato

I think new baby potatoes work especially well with this recipe but you could use baked potatoes or possibly roast potatoes. But babies work best for me.

Cumin and Coriander Salmon

Serves 4

This is a quick and simple dish to make yet it tastes so good it would make a great dinner option when you have guests over.

INSTRUCTIONS

Put the cumin and coriander seeds in a pestle and mortar and grind until mostly crushed. Sprinkle evenly over the salmon and press down.

To make the dressing add the sesame oil to a pan along with the fish sauce, chilli sauce, lime juice, honey and water and warm through gently. Stir to mix until the honey dissolves. Taste and add a little bit more of any of the dressing ingredients if needed to balance out the flavours.

To cook the salmon you can either shallow fry it with a touch of oil for approximately 2-3 minutes on each side until cooked to your liking. Alternatively you could wrap the salmon in tin foil and bake in the oven for about 10 minutes. Either way times can change depending how you like your fish cooked and the size of the fillets.

When you are ready to serve, put the rocket into the middle of your plate and place on the salmon. Slice your sun dried tomatoes into strips and lay them on top of the salmon. Finally drizzle the dressing all over the dish.

INGREDIENTS

Splash of Olive Oil
2 Seabass Fillets with flour to dust
1 small Onion, finely chopped
2 Garlic Cloves, finely chopped
3 medium Tomatoes, chopped
2 Carrots, diced into small squares
3 tbsp Bacon Bits or small pack
pancetta, fried
1 pint Chicken Stock
1 Tin of Beans (such as Cannellini)
Pinch of Salt and Pepper
Squeeze of Lemon Juice

*You can bulk this out by adding a side
portion of vegetables. Greens like broccoli
work well with this. You can also change
up the fish but I think a white fish works
best with the beans.*

Seabass and Beans

Serves 2 (can easily be doubled)

This is one of Andrew's favourite dinners. We have been making it forever. Really quick to prepare, healthy and tastes really good. It is a weeknight staple for us.

INSTRUCTIONS

Add the oil to a pan and sauté the onions until they soften. Then add the garlic and stir for a few more minutes. Add the chopped tomato and stir until the tomato goes all "mushy" and becomes a sauce. Add the carrot, bacon bits (or fried pancetta if using) and the chicken stock. Bring to a boil then reduce to a simmer and cook gently until the vegetables are just starting to go soft. If more water is needed just top up as you go.

There should still be extra liquid at this stage so now is the time to drain, rinse and add the beans to the pan (although it is fine to just add the beans direct from the tin I think by rinsing them you wash away excess salt which is not needed). Stir then carry on cooking for about another 10 minutes while the beans absorb all the flavours.

It is ready when the carrots are soft and the excess liquid has evaporated to leave behind a yummy bacon"y" pan of beans which should be the consistency of baked beans (but way more tasty).

Just before the beans are ready add salt and pepper to your flour then dust the fish lightly. Add a splash of olive oil to a frying pan then fry the fish for about 2 minutes each side depending on the thickness of the fish. As soon as the fish is cooked through squeeze over some lemon juice into the pan before removing and serving with the beans.

INGREDIENTS

Splash of Olive Oil
1 Onion, finely chopped
2 Garlic Cloves, finely chopped
8 Roma Tomatoes, chopped
Small glass of White Wine
4 tbsp of Bacon Bits or a small pack
of Pancetta
120g crumbled Feta Cheese
32 medium sized Raw Prawns, peeled
Squeeze of Lemon Juice
2 tbsp Parsley, chopped
400g of Pasta of choice (we like
spaghetti or tagliatelle with this dish)

NOTE

If you are using pancetta instead of the
bacon bits fry them in the pan along
with the onions before adding in the
garlic and tomatoes.

*You could substitute cream for the feta
here or add chicken instead of prawns.
This would also be a great vegetarian dish
by leaving out the prawns and bacon and
adding something like peas or broccoli as
the sauce is just as tasty all by itself!*

Prawn and Feta Pasta

Serves 4

I just sort of made this recipe up one night when I had some left over feta and it was really tasty. I have made it hundreds of times since. Just don't forget to remove the intestine artery before cooking the prawns as they can be gritty.

INSTRUCTIONS

Start by cooking your pasta according to the packet instructions, which is normally between 10—15 minutes, or to the texture your like your pasta.

While the pasta is cooking add the oil to a pan and sauté the onions for about 5 minutes until they soften. Then add the garlic and bacon bits and fry for a few more minutes. Now add the chopped tomatoes and white wine and cook until the tomatoes become mushy and broken down in a sauce.

Once the tomato mixture is ready add the feta and cook until melted. Turn down the heat to low and add in the prawns and cook until they turn from grey to pink which should only take around 2-3 minutes. Keep an eye on them as you do not want to over cook them as they will go chewy.

While the prawns are cooking drain your pasta reserving a mug full of the water in case it is needed for the final sauce consistency. Now add the parsley and lemon juice to your prawn sauce along with the drained pasta. At this stage add a little bit of that pasta water to loosen if too thick.

INGREDIENTS

Salmon
4 Salmon Fillets
1 tbsp Chilli Powder
2 tbsp Oregano
1 tbsp Curry Powder
1 tbsp Cumin Seeds
1 tbsp Garlic Powder

Sweetcorn Salsa
2 Cobbs of fresh Corn
2 medium Tomatoes, diced
3 Spring Onions, chopped
½ Red Chilli, chopped (add more or less depending on heat preference)
Juice of 1 Lime
Sprinkle of Salt and Pepper
Handful of fresh Coriander, chopped

Tomato and Mustard Salsa
4 medium fresh Tomatoes, diced
1 tbsp Wholegrain Mustard
½ Red Onion, finely chopped
Juice of 1 Lime
Splash of Olive Oil
Sprinkle of Salt and Pepper
Handful of fresh Coriander, chopped

I serve both these dishes with rice and peas. I also like to add a side portion of guacamole when the mood takes me. I usually go down that route when making the sweetcorn salsa especially.

Spicy Salmon with Salsa Two Ways

Serves 4

This is a light yet really flavoursome mid-week supper. Choose either of the two salsas depending on your preference. Or if you are feeling really out there serve them both!!

INSTRUCTIONS

Heat Oven to 400°F / 200 °C / Gas Mark 6

Firstly make your salsa (s) to give all the flavours a chance to combine. If making the sweetcorn salsa start by grilling the corn in a dry frying pan until lightly seared all over. Once cool enough to handle cut the corn off the cobb and add to a bowl. Add in the rest of the ingredients and stir. Taste and add more seasoning if required or even extra lime juice.

If making the tomato salsa simply mix all the ingredients together, again adding extra seasoning if required and more lime juice as needed.

Once the salsa is prepared refrigerate until ready to serve. Now mix together all the spices in a bowl and coat evenly over the salmon fillets. Wrap them in tin foil and bake in the oven until just cooked, approximately 10 minutes depending on the size of the salmon.

INGREDIENTS

For the Base
1 Onion, finely chopped
3 tbsp White Wine Vinegar
150ml White Wine
200ml Double Cream
2 large Fillets of any White Fish,
chopped into bite sized pieced
200g of Raw Prawns, peeled
12 Scallops (optional)
500g bag of fresh Spinach

For the Topping
200ml Milk (any type)
2 Garlic Cloves
½ Red Chilli
Pinch of Saffron (optional)
Around 2lb Potatoes (or enough for four
people), peeled and cubed
1 Lemon, zested and juiced

*You could also serve these in individual
dishes if you wanted to make a statement
for a dinner party for instance. Serve with
a green salad in the centre of the table.
Your guests will be impressed.*

Funky Fish Pie

Serves 4

I have given a traditional fish pie a bit of "zing" to jazz it up so it's
not the norm. I love the subtleness of the lemon, saffron and chilli
flavour in the mash topping. Add more or less to suit your taste.

INSTRUCTIONS

Heat Oven to 400°F / 200 °C / Gas Mark 6

Add the onion, white wine vinegar and white wine to a saucepan and cook on
a medium heat until the onions have softened and the liquid has reduced by
half. Then add the cream, mix together and leave aside to cool.

Add the garlic and chilli to a pestle and mortar and mash to a pulp. Scrap
into a saucepan and add the milk and saffron. Bring to a simmer then remove
from the heat and leave to infuse.

Boil the potatoes until soft then drain and mash. Then add the infused milk
mixture, the zest and the juice of the lemon and give it a good mix. Wilt the
spinach by putting it in a colander and pouring over boiling water. Then rinse
with cold water so it is easy to handle. Remove from the colander and
squeeze out any excess water. Finely chop the spinach and set aside.

Add the white fish, prawns and scallops to the cream mixture, mix then tip
into a casserole dish. Top evenly with the chopped spinach then spread over
the mash. Cook the pie for around 30-50 minutes or until bubbling around
the edges, starting to brown and completely cooked through.

INGREDIENTS

For the Base
1 Onion, finely chopped
100g Butter
50g Flour
1 pint of Milk
500g Smoked Haddock
250g bag of Raw Prawns
1 tbsp Capers (optional)
2 hard-boiled Eggs, roughly chopped
3 tbsp fresh Parsley, finely chopped
1 tbsp Lemon Juice
Pinch of Salt and Pepper

For the Topping
Around 2lb Potatoes (or enough
for four people)
A good knob of Butter
4 tbsp Milk
25g Cheddar Cheese, grated

NOTE
Any type of fish can be used in this
recipe. Just whatever you have to hand
or is sustainably available. For special
occasions try adding in scallops or a
mixture of white fish and haddock.

*This is a hearty meal so we normally serve
it on its own. However, you could serve
alongside green vegetables such as peas,
broccoli or asparagus. If serving to my
Dad it is a must that it is served with
chips!!*

Fish Pie

Serves 4

This is comfort food on a plate. It is a traditional recipe that never fails to make you feel satisfied and content. A bit like somebody just gave you a big warm HUG!

INSTRUCTIONS

Heat Oven to 400°F / 200 °C / Gas Mark 6

Make the topping first by peeling and boiling the potatoes. Once they are soft drain them and use a potato masher to mash up the potatoes until you have no lumps.

Add the butter, milk, cheddar cheese and continue mashing until it is all combined. Set aside.

Add the onions and butter to a pan and cook on a medium heat until the onions have softened. Then add the flour and stir for a few minutes to cook it out. Now slowly add the milk, bit by bit (to avoid it going lumpy) until you have a thick and creamy white sauce consistency. Take it off the heat and leave to cool.

Cut the haddock into bite sized pieces and set aside. Peel and de-vein the prawns.

Once the sauce has cooled add in the haddock, prawns, capers, chopped eggs, parsley, lemon juice and salt and pepper and give it a good stir. Pour the mixture into a casserole dish and cover evenly with the mash topping.

Cook for around 40 minutes or until the top is golden brown and the pie is oozing out the filling around the edges.

INGREDIENTS

4 Seabass Fillets
Flour for dusting
Splash of Olive Oil
1 Onion, finely chopped
2 Garlic Cloves, finely chopped
¼ red Chilli, finely chopped
Splash of White Wine
300g Cherry Tomatoes, halved
2 tsp Oregano
2 tbsp Capers
12 Black Olives, pitted and halved
Handful fresh Parsley, finely chopped
Pinch of Salt and Pepper

*I like to serve this recipe with herbed new
potatoes. I just par boil the potatoes,
drain then add them to a frying pan along
with a splash of olive oil, some rosemary,
salt and pepper and cook for about 10
minutes until they start to brown and are
soft all the way through.*

Seabass Provençale

Serves 4

This is a great mid-week supper as it takes very little time to prepare or to cook yet it still delivers on flavour. You can substitute the seabass for any white fish or even salmon or tuna. To be fair the sauce would be tasty on anything!

INSTRUCTIONS

On a medium heat fry the onion in the oil for around 5-10 minutes or until softened. Add the garlic and chilli and continue to cook for a few more minutes. Now add in the wine, tomatoes and oregano and cook down for 5 more minutes until the alcohol has evaporated.

While the sauce is cooking dust the seabass fillets with some seasoned flour then add to a lightly oiled frying pan. Cook on each side for approximately 2-3 minutes depending on size. Once fully cooked it can be placed on the serving dish ready for the sauce.

At this stage add the capers, olives and parsley to the sauce pan and stir until warmed through which should just take a couple more minutes. Season with salt and pepper and serve over the cooked fish.

INGREDIENTS

4 Cod Fillets
Flour for dusting
Pinch of Salt and Pepper
Splash of Olive Oil
2 Red Peppers
150g Sun-Dried Tomatoes
½ red Chilli (optional)
50g Black Olives, pitted
2 Garlic Cloves
1 tbsp Oregano
Squeeze of Lemon Juice (optional)

Even if you do not like olives please give this a try as the flavour completely changes with the pepper and tomatoes. I like to serve this recipe with either a baked potato or new potatoes alongside a vegetable such as purple sprouting broccoli.

Cod with Red Pepper Tapenade

Serves 4

This can be made with any type of fish but I prefer using a white fish as I feel the flavours of the tapenade are quite intense (yet delicious) and so work better than with an oily fish like salmon.

INSTRUCTIONS

Arrange the peppers on a baking tray (I line mine with foil first) and place them under the grill for around 10 minutes. Make sure you turn them over at regular intervals until the pepper is cooked and charred all the way around. It may look burnt but this is totally fine as the skin will be coming off.

Once the pepper is charred all over remove from the grill and place into a sealed plastic bag and set aside for around 15 minutes or until they are cool enough to handle. As soon as they are ready take them out of the bag and remove the skins discarding the seeds and any pith but trying to keep as much of the juices as possible.

Add the cooked peppers to a food processor along with the sun-dried tomatoes, chilli (if using), olives, garlic and oregano. Give it a good blitz until lovely and smooth. Check for seasoning.

At this point you can start on the fish by dusting the fillets with some seasoned flour and adding to a lightly oiled frying pan. Cook on each side for approximately 2-3 minutes depending on size. Once fully cooked drizzle over the lemon juice and serve alongside the warm tapenade.

INGREDIENTS

800g Cod Fillet, cubed
16 large Prawns, peeled
4 Rosemary Sprigs,
2 Garlic Cloves, crushed
4 tbsp Olive Oil
Juice of a Lemon
30g Parmesan Cheese, grated
30g Panko Breadcrumbs
Pinch of Salt and Pepper

This could be served with mash or new potatoes alongside some vegetables. It would also be mighty scrumptious served on its own with a whole load of crusty bread and butter to mop up the juices.

Cod and Prawn Bake

Serves 4

Monkfish would make a great alternative for this dish as it is such a meaty fish. You could also add additional seafood such as scallops which would really "posh it up".

INSTRUCTIONS

Heat Oven to 400°F / 200 °C / Gas Mark 6

Take the leaves off the rosemary and finely chop them before putting into a bowl. Add in the garlic, oil and lemon juice along with the cod and prawns and give it a good mix. Leave the fish to marinade for around an hour giving it a stir now and again to make sure the fish gets marinated evenly.

Once ready to cook transfer the mixture, including the marinade to an oven-proof casserole dish which fits the fish in snuggly, ensuring everything is level. Mix together the breadcrumbs, parmesan, salt and pepper and sprinkle over the top making sure it is all covered well.

Bake in the oven for around 20-30 minutes or until the fish is cooked all the way through and the top has started bubbling and turning a lovely golden brown.

INGREDIENTS

1 ½ lb large, Raw Prawns
4 large Tomatillos
1 Onion, cut into ¼ chunks
1 Green Pepper, cut into ¼ chunks
1 Jalapeno Pepper, seeds removed
3 Garlic Cloves
Large handful of Coriander Stems
1 Chicken Stock Cube
200g Basmati Rice
Splash of Olive Oil
Pinch of Salt and Pepper

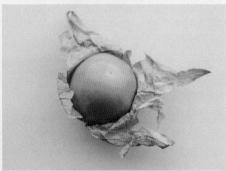

I like to make this recipe for a really light lunch by just leaving out the rice. It really reduces the cooking time as you do not need to wait for the rice to cook and you end up with a sort of thick prawn soup. I LOVE the tangy flavour combination.

Tomatillo Prawns

Serves 4

I came across this recipe while living in Texas where they use a lot of tomatillos due to the closeness of Mexico where they use them in many Mexican recipes and sauces. Whole tomatillos are a fruit, closest in taste to a green unripe tomato. Tomatillos are also known as fresadilla or Mexican green tomatoes. If you cannot find fresh tomatillos then canned would work in this recipe.

INSTRUCTIONS

Peel and wash the tomatillos then cut them in half. Add them to a food processor along with ½ the onion, ¼ of the green pepper, the jalapeno pepper, the garlic cloves and the coriander stems and blitz to a puree.

Finely chop the remaining onion and green pepper and using a splash of oil fry them on a medium heat for around 5-10 minutes or until softened. Add the tomatillo puree and continue to cook for around 5 more minutes or until the sauce has thickened. At this point add in a pint of water along with the chicken stock cube and bring to a boil.

Add in the rice and cover. Reduce the heat to low and cook for a further 15 minutes or until the rice is cooked. If the liquid reduces too much just add extra water to top it up. For the finished dish you are looking for a sort of stew consistency. When the rice is cooked add in the prawns, give it a good stir, replace the lid and turn off the heat. Let it stand for 5 minutes or until the prawns have turned pink all over and are cooked through. Taste and add salt and pepper as required.

INGREDIENTS

1 lb Pork Mince
1 Onion, finely chopped
Thumb sized piece of Ginger, grated
2 Garlic Cloves, crushed
425g tin of good Chicken Stock
3 tbsp Soy Sauce
4 Pak Choi
1 tbsp Chilli Garlic Sauce (add more
or less depending on taste)
3 Spring Onions, chopped
4 Egg Noodle Nests
Squeeze of Lime Juice
Chopped Coriander to garnish

You could substitute the pork mince with chicken or turkey mince or even beef mince although I prefer the pork mince as it is full of flavour and much lighter. Note that if you have extra pork mixture left over it freezes really well however, I would not freeze it once you have added the noodles as it goes quite stodgy.

Chinese Pork Noodles

Serves 4

A warming bowl of deliciousness and it's super healthy and quick to make. If you don't have Pak Choi just substitute it for any other vegetables you might have in the fridge.

INSTRUCTIONS

Add the pork mince to the pan and sauté until it turns brown all over. Now add the onions, ginger and garlic and stir for 5 minutes. Add the chicken stock and soy sauce and simmer for 15 minutes or until the pork and onions soften.

At this stage add the pak choi, spring onions (reserve the greens) and chilli garlic sauce and stir. Cook for a further 5 minutes then squeeze in the lime juice. Add as much or as little as you like according to your personal taste. At the same time put your noodles in boiling water and cook as per the instructions (normally around 3-5 minutes). Once the noodles are cooked drain them and add to your serving bowl. Spoon the pork mixture over the noodles and garnish with the coriander and the chopped greens from the spring onions. Serve with extra soy sauce or lime juice if needed.

INGREDIENTS

Splash of Olive Oil
1 Onion, finely chopped
3 Carrots, chopped into cubes
2 sticks of Celery, chopped
2 Garlic Cloves, chopped
2lb Pork Loin, cubed
1 tsp Parsley and Rosemary
1 tsp Sage and Thyme
1 Chicken Stock Cube
2 Sausages (any type)
2 Smoked Sausage Links
1 Red Pepper, diced
4 Tomatoes, chopped
425g tin Cannellini Beans
425g tin Flageolet Beans
Glass of White Wine
3 tbsp chopped Parsley

I serve this in wide bowls along with lots and lots of crusty bread and of course butter. You can easily cook it in advance and just re-heat when you are ready to eat.

Pork and Bean Casserole

Serves 4

This is a perfect dish for feeding a crowd as the ingredients are relatively cheap yet it is still tasty and satisfying. The preparation time is super fast although it does take a few hours to cook. It can be made in the slow cooker or on the hob.

INSTRUCTIONS

Add the oil to the pan along with the onions, carrots and celery and sauté for a few minutes. Now add the garlic and stir for 2 more minutes. Add the pork and herbs and approximately 1 pint of water. Add the chicken stock cube and bring to a boil. Put the lid on, reduce the heat and simmer for about an hour (2 hours if using a slow cooker). Stir occasionally and top up with water if needed.

While this is cooking prepare the sausages by sealing them in a pan until brown all over. Remove and let cool and when able to handle cut them into coins about 2cm thick. Cut the smoked sausage links to the same thickness.

When the casserole has been cooking for an hour add the red pepper, sausages, tomatoes and white wine. Drain and rinse the beans and add them to the casserole as well. Check water levels again and top up if needed. Put the lid back on and continue to cook for another hour (2 hours if using a slow cooker). Stir occasionally and top up with water if needed. Once the pork is soft and falling apart and you have a medium thickness consistency it is done. Add in the parsley and stir then you are ready to serve.

INGREDIENTS

Splash of Olive Oil
4 boneless Chicken Thighs
1 Onion, quartered
3 Garlic Cloves, crushed
1 thumb sized piece of Ginger, grated
Juice of 1 Lime
1 tsp of each Cumin, Turmeric and
Chilli Powder
1 pack of fresh Coriander, chopped
400ml can of reduced-fat Coconut Milk
½ Red Chilli, chopped (add more or less
depending on heat preference)
1 Chicken Stock Cube

I serve this with basmati rice and naan bread. You can serve it with my favourite side portion of Spicy Green Beans (recipe shown in the sides section) but I don't think it actually needs it on this occasion as it is so light unlike the meatier curries.

Scrummy Chicken Curry

Serves 4

This recipe tastes even nicer if you marinade it the night before but it is not essential. Just marinade as long as you can. I use chicken thighs because I feel they have more flavour but you can just as easily substitute with chicken breasts.

INSTRUCTIONS

Cut the chicken into thumb sized chunks and place in a bowl. Add the chilli powder, garlic, ginger, the lime juice and half the chopped coriander. Stir well and leave to marinade for as long as you can.

When ready to cook, add the onion to a food processor and blitz to a puree. Tip this into a pan along with the splash of oil and fry gently until starting to soften. This should take between 5 and 10 minutes. Now add the cumin and turmeric and stir well for a further 1 minute.

At this stage add the chicken and its marinade and cook until the chicken changes colour. Then add the coconut milk, the fresh chilli and the chicken stock cube. Stir and bring to the boil before reducing the heat to a simmer. Cover the pan with a lid and leave to cook gently for about 20 minutes or until the chicken is cooked through. If the curry sauce becomes too thick just add a little water as you go if needed. Add the remaining coriander, stir and it is ready to eat.

INGREDIENTS

Splash of Olive Oil
1 Onion, finely chopped
2 Garlic Cloves, finely chopped
300g Arborio Rice
Large glass of White Wine
1 Chicken Stock Cube
2 Chicken Breasts, cubed
150g Frozen Peas
100g Parmesan Cheese, grated
Squeeze of Lemon Juice (optional)

NOTE
There are so many ways to change up risotto. Try adding artichokes, broccoli, courgettes, mushrooms, pesto, bacon, sausage, chorizo, or prawns. You can change the cheese up too. Try stilton, cheddar, mascarpone or a mixture. The list is endless – just make it your own.

I often make this risotto but leave out the chicken and replace it with a mixture of chopped porcini mushrooms and fresh mushrooms. I use the liquid that the porcini mushrooms steep in to add a deeper earthy flavour. I fry sliced fresh mushrooms and add them at the end of cooking.

Chicken and Pea Risotto

Serves 4

We all like risotto. It is just so velvety, cheesy and rich. The way I make risotto it is not hard like they say on the TV. You do have to stir regularly during cooking but there is something I find very therapeutic about that I have to say!

INSTRUCTIONS

Firstly put a full kettle of water on to boil. While it is boiling sauté the onions in a pan with the oil until the onions start to soften. Then add the garlic and fry for a few more minutes. Now add the rice and stir to ensure it is fully coated. Add the wine and reduce down by half.

Once the kettle has boiled pour approximately 1 litre of the water into a pan, add the stock cube and stir. Leave it on the hob on a super low heat. It is now time to add the stock to the rice. Add one ladle of hot stock at a time. Stir it until all the liquid has absorbed then add another ladle of stock. Stir again until that has been absorbed. Keep doing the same thing again and again until the rice is cooked to your liking (it should be cooked El Dente but we prefer it with no bite). This takes around 20 minutes. If you run out of stock before the rice is cooked just keep topping up with hot water.

Once the rice is nearly ready add in the chicken and cook for 5 minutes or until fully cooked through. Finish off by adding the peas, parmesan and a squeeze of lemon juice (if using) and cook for a further couple of minutes until the peas have warmed through and the cheese has melted.

INGREDIENTS

Splash of Olive Oil
4 Chicken Thighs (or breasts)
1 Onion, finely chopped
3 Garlic Cloves, crushed
1 thumb sized piece of Ginger, grated
½ Red Chilli, chopped (add more or
less depending on heat preference)
1 tbsp of each Cumin and Coriander
1 tsp Turmeric and Chilli Powder
1 tsp de-podded Cardamom Seeds
1 Cinnamon Stick
400ml can Chopped Tomatoes
1 Chicken Stock Cube
1 tbsp Mango Chutney
4 fresh or dried Lime Leaves

*I serve this with basmati rice and a side
portion of naan bread and sometimes I
also make Spicy Green Beans (the recipes
for both the naan and green beans are in
my sides section). It freezes really well so
even if I am only cooking for two I still
make the recipe for 4 people and freeze
the left overs for a quick Friday night
treat.*

Tomato Chicken Curry

Serves 4

Whoever says curries are not healthy are WRONG. This recipe
does not take long to prepare and is super healthy yet still very
yummy.

INSTRUCTIONS

Add a splash of oil to a pan along with the onions and fry gently until starting
to soften. This should take between 5 and 10 minutes. Add the garlic,
ginger and chilli and fry for a few more minutes.

Now add in all your spices and stir well for a further 1 minute. At this stage
you can add the tin of tomatoes along with a tin of water, the chicken stock
cube, mango chutney and the lime leaves.

Add in the chicken, stir and bring to the boil. Reduce the heat down to a
simmer and cook for about 30 minutes or until the chicken is tender and the
sauce is nicely thick.

When it is ready remove the chicken from the pan and when cool enough to
handle cut it into bite sized pieces then replace back in the sauce and give it
a good stir. It is now ready to serve.

INGREDIENTS

Splash of Olive Oil
4 Chicken Breasts
8 oz ball fresh Mozzarella, sliced
1 punnet Cherry Tomatoes
1 tsp Garlic Salt
Pinch of Salt, Pepper and Thyme
2 cups of Rocket

For the Pesto:
Large handful of Basil and Parsley
3 tbsp Mint Leaves
6 tbsp Parmesan Cheese
1 large Garlic Clove
4 tbsp of Olive Oil

Veg Option – substitute a thick slice of aubergine for the chicken. Cook in a similar way but fry the aubergine on both sides before adding the pesto and mozzarella.

I like to serve this dish with baby new potatoes but a baked potato would work just as well. Just out of interest the roasted cherry tomatoes go really well on the side on a Sunday brunch (only for me though as the rest of the family are not a fan of fresh roast tomatoes on anything!

Pesto Chicken

Serves 4

This is a simple mid-week supper that will have your taste buds tingling. You could make it even more scrumptious by breading the chicken but to be honest it is just as nice as it is.

INSTRUCTIONS

Firstly make the pesto by adding all the ingredients to a food processor and blitz until it becomes the consistency of a puree.

Place the cherry tomatoes in an oven proof dish and sprinkle over a touch of oil, the garlic salt, thyme, salt and pepper. Give it a good mix then roast in the oven for approximately 20 minutes or until they are turning golden and just starting to pop.

While the tomatoes are cooking place the chicken breasts in between plastic wrap or in a plastic bag and give it a bang with a rolling pin to flatten it out a little. Sprinkle with salt and pepper.

Add a splash of oil to a frying pan and cook the chicken for 2-3 minutes on a medium heat. Now turn the chicken over and top with the pesto and slices of mozzarella. Cover the pan with a lid and cook for another 3 minutes or until the chicken is cooked all the way through and the cheese has melted.

To serve place the chicken on a plate alongside the cherry tomatoes and top with the rocket.

INGREDIENTS

5 Tortilla Wraps
Splash of Olive Oil
1 Onion, finely chopped
2 Garlic Cloves, finely chopped
1 Red Pepper, finely chopped
400g tin Chopped Tomatoes
2 tbsp Coriander Stalks, finely chopped
½ Red Chilli, finely chopped (optional)
Pinch of Salt and Pepper
2 x 400g Tinned Beans
4 Chicken Thighs, cooked and shredded
150g Frozen Sweetcorn
125g Cheddar Cheese, grated

NOTE
You can use any beans you like for this recipe. Cannellini, Kidney or Black Beans work well. I like to use a mixture of dark and light beans for colour. You can also substitute chicken breast if you prefer.

I like to serve this in pizza style slices as we cook it in a round casserole dish but feel free to serve any way you like. We have it alongside a side portion of salad or sometimes an avocado type salsa. But if I am honest that's only for me. The boys just have it as it comes!!

Tortilla Lasagne
Makes approximately 4 medium size portions

I came across this recipe in a cookbook but as a vegetarian version. Of course feeding a very "non vegetarian" family I decided to keep them happy by adding cooked chicken. It still keeps it tasty but adds the protein the boys crave. A Great decision made.

INSTRUCTIONS

Heat Oven to 400°F / 200 °C / Gas Mark 6

Place the oil in a pan and sauté the onions, red pepper and chilli (if using) until softened. Then add the garlic and cook for a few more minutes. Add the tin of chopped tomatoes along with a tin full of water. Add the coriander stalks, salt and pepper and bring to a boil. Once boiling reduce to a simmer and cook until the sauce becomes thick and resembles a sort of pasta sauce consistency. Once ready leave to cool.

Meanwhile prepare the filling by rinsing the beans in a colander to remove all the salt and starchy stuff. Then add to a bowl along with the sweetcorn, cheese and the shredded cooked chicken.

When the sauce has cooled add this to the bean mixture. Give it a good stir and you are now ready to make your lasagne. Start with a round casserole dish the same size as the tortillas. Now begin with a small layer of bean mixture on the bottom of the casserole dish so the first tortilla doesn't stick. Then just layer tortilla then beans, tortilla then beans until the last top layer is the bean mixture. You can sprinkle over extra cheese on top if you like.

Bake in the oven for approximately 30 minutes until it is brown and bubbling. Once cooked cover and let it rest for 5 minutes before serving.

INGREDIENTS

Splash of Olive Oil
4 large boneless Chicken Thighs
2 Carrots, cut into large cubes
2 Onions, cut into large cubes
1 Red Pepper, cut into large cubes
4 Garlic Cloves, cut into large cubes
500g New Potatoes, cut in half
2 tsp of each Paprika and Rosemary
3 tbsp of Bacon Bits or pack of Pancetta
2 tbsp Honey
Juice of a Lemon
Pinch of Salt and Pepper

This can easily be changed up by just adding any vegetables you might happen to have left in the fridge. It can be served just as it is on its own or why not add a side portion of fresh vegetables or even a nice slice of crusty bread and butter!!

Easy Peasy One Pot Chicken

Serves 4

I came across this recipe years ago and could not get over how simple and quick it was to make yet still has a ton of flavour going on. I passed on the recipe to my Mum and she still makes it all the time in her house even to this day.

INSTRUCTIONS

Heat Oven to 400°F / 200 °C / Gas Mark 6

Par boil the potatoes for approximately 5 minutes then drain. Add them to a casserole dish along with all the other ingredients (except the honey). Give it a good stir and bake for 30 minutes.

After 30 minutes take it out of the oven, add the honey and give it another stir. Cook for a further 15-30 minutes or until all the vegetables are soft and the chicken is cooked through.

It is now ready. How simple was that??

INGREDIENTS

8 boneless Chicken Thighs
1 Onion, finely chopped
3 tbsp Bacon Bits or
small pack pancetta, fried
2 Carrots, cut into small cubes
4 Garlic Cloves, finely chopped
2 tsp Paprika
1 Bay Leaf
1 tsp Garlic Powder
1 tbsp Red Wine Vinegar
1 400g tin of Chopped Tomatoes
1 Chicken Stock Cube
12 Green Olives (optional)
Pinch of Salt and Pepper

NOTE
I like to cook this in the slow cooker as
you can just throw everything in, turn it
on and leave it until you are ready to
eat. But you can easily make it on the
hob by putting all the ingredients in a
pan, bringing it to the boil then
reducing to a simmer. Cover and cook
for around 1 hour or until the chicken is
falling off the bone and the vegetables
are soft.

*You could add green vegetables like Kale
to this recipe for even more goodness or
you could add a tin of
beans such as cannellini to bulk it out.
I like to serve it with either rice or new
potatoes and a side portion of vegetables
such as broccoli.*

Chicken Cacciatore

Serves 4

This is one of my favourite ways to eat chicken. I love tomatoes
and all the flavours just sing together. Very tasty and good for
you at the same time. What could be better?

INSTRUCTIONS

Add all the ingredients into a slow cooker. Fill the empty tomato can half
way up with water and add that as well. If you have a saute setting bring it
to the boil. If not just add all the ingredients to a pan, bring to the boil then
add back into the slow cooker.

Set the slow cooker for 4 hours then leave it to do its magic. Once cooking
time is over just check the vegetables are soft before serving.

INGREDIENTS

1 large pack of pancetta
1 Onion, finely chopped
2 Leeks, sliced into half moons
3 Carrots, cut into cubes
½ tsp dried Mint
1 Lemon, zested
3 Garlic Cloves, finely chopped
300g Puy Lentils
1 tsp English Mustard
1 tsp Wholegrain Mustard
1 Chicken Stock Cube
4 small Chicken Breast
3 tbsp fresh Parsley, chopped
Pinch of Salt and Pepper
Squeeze of Lemon Juice (optional)

This a meal in itself but you could also serve it with a side portion of vegetables or for those winter nights some crusty bread would go down a treat. This could easily be converted to a vegetarian main by missing out the chicken. The flavours are so tasty that it would still hold its own!

Chicken with Lentils and Bacon

Serves 4

I love lentils and this one pan wonder is so easy to make and tastes really delicious plus it is warm and filling. It goes down a treat in our house any time of the year.

INSTRUCTIONS

Fry the pancetta in a pan along with the onion, leeks, carrots, mint and the lemon zest. Cook on a medium heat for about 10 minutes or until the vegetables start to soften. Now add the garlic and cook for a few more minutes.

Stir in the lentils and mustards. Now add 1000ml of water and the chicken stock cube and give it a stir. Bring to the boil then put the lid on and reduce to a simmer. Cook for approximately 15 minutes or until the lentils are just starting to soften. Cut the chicken into small cubes then add to the pan and continue to cook for a further 10 minutes or until the chicken is cooked through, the lentils are nice and tender and the sauce has thickened. While cooking stir occasionally and add extra water if it becomes too dry before the lentils cook through.

Once ready add the parsley (leave a tablespoon for garnish) and season with salt and pepper as needed. I also like to add a squeeze of fresh lemon juice at this stage but this is totally optional depending on your taste. Add to your serving bowl and sprinkle with the remaining tablespoon of parsley.

INGREDIENTS

4 Chicken Breasts
1 Lime, juiced
2 thumb-sized pieces of Ginger, grated
1 Garlic Clove, grated
½ Red Chilli, finely chopped
2 tbsp Honey
2 tbsp Soy Sauce
1 tbsp Worcestershire Sauce
Handful of fresh Coriander, chopped
Splash of Sesame Oil
4 Spring Onions, sliced
2 tbsp Sesame Seeds

I like to serve this with guacamole which can be made by smashing up an avocado in a bowl then adding some chopped tomatoes and a chopped spring onion along with a good squeeze of lime juice before stirring to combine.

You could also add a side portion of sweet potatoes cut into wedges, coated with a spicy jerk seasoning and a bit of olive oil, then roasted. I think the flavour combination of the Chinese chicken, the soft zingy guacamole and the spicy sweet potatoes work really well together.

Chinese Chicken Strips

Serves 4

This is a great dinner than can be put together in no time at all and with hardly any washing up as you marinade the chicken in the same pan you are going to fry it in! It is a "grown up" version of chicken tenders but way more tasty.

INSTRUCTIONS

Slice the chicken into 2cm strips and set aside. Now add all the remaining ingredients (except the spring onions and sesame seeds) to a frying pan and mix together. Add in the chicken and give it a good stir to ensure it is fully coated. Set aside to marinade for approximately 1-2 hours.

When ready to prepare simply place the frying pan on a medium heat and cook the chicken for about 2-3 minutes on each side or until it is fully cooked through. Place on your serving plate and scatter over the spring onions and sesame seeds.

INGREDIENTS

Splash of Olive Oil
40g dried Porcini Mushrooms
200g fresh mushrooms, sliced
1 Onion, thinly diced
3 Garlic Cloves, crushed
700g Pork Fillet, thinly sliced
3 tbsp Brandy
2 tsp Paprika
½ tsp Cayenne Pepper
2 tsp Dijon Mustard
150ml Chicken Stock
200ml Crème Fresh (Sour Cream
can be substituted)
1 Lemon, juiced
2 tbsp fresh Parsley, chopped
A pinch of Salt and Pepper

I serve this with a flavoured rice. Simply fry some chopped onion, red pepper and crushed garlic until soft then add in the rice along with chicken or vegetable stock to cover about an inch over the top of the rice. Bring to the boil and cook for a few minutes before turning off the heat and putting the lid on. Leave for about 15 minutes or until the rice is tender and the water has evaporated.

Pork and Mushroom Stroganoff
Serves 4

Steak or chicken can easily be substituted for the pork for an alternative meal option. It is so tasty that it would make a great vegetarian meal too by just missing out the pork all together as the porcini give it a real meaty richness. Serve with rice or pasta.

INSTRUCTIONS

Cover the porcini mushrooms with 200ml of boiling water and leave to soak for a minimum of 30 minutes to re-hydrate. Once ready squeeze out the excess liquid and finely chop the mushrooms, reserving the soaking liquid.

Add the olive oil and fresh mushrooms to a frying pan and cook on a high heat for about 5 minutes until they brown. Reduce the heat down to a medium and add in the onions and cook for a further 10 minutes or until they are starting to soften. Then add the garlic and pork and cook for a further 2 minutes.

At this point add in the brandy and ignite to flambé it burning off the alcohol. Now add the chopped porcini mushrooms, paprika, cayenne, mustard, chicken stock, crème fresh and the liquid from the porcini mushrooms (be careful not to let the gritty bits at the bottom go in).

Bring to a simmer then cook uncovered for about 5 minutes or until you have a creamy consistency. Add in a squeeze of lemon juice along with the parsley and stir. Season with salt and pepper if required.

INGREDIENTS

8 good quality Sausages
1 Onion, finely chopped
1 Garlic Clove, finely chopped
1 Apple, peeled and cubed
2 tbsp Wholegrain Mustard
1 Chicken Stock Cube
1 tbsp Redcurrant Jelly
1 Fresh Rosemary Sprig, stripped
and chopped

When making this recipe I tend to cook a little longer than needed so that the apple disappears into the sauce but that is only because Andrew is not a big fan of fruit in hot food. We like to serve it with mashed potatoes and a side of vegetables (although vegetables are not needed here, I just like to add them to most evening meals I make!!).

Sausage and Apple One Pot Wonder

Serves 4

The flavours in this recipe are really delicious and work so well together. It is easy to prepare and makes a great family meal for any night of the week. You can replace the fresh rosemary with dried and choose whichever sausages float your boat.

INSTRUCTIONS

Add the sausages to a deep sided frying pan and brown on all sides over a medium heat. Once coloured remove them from the pan and set aside. If needed add a splash of oil then add the onion and garlic to the same pan and cook for another 5 minutes or so until the onions become soft.

Add 300ml of water along with the apple, mustard, stock cube, redcurrant jelly and rosemary and give it a good stir until combined. Then add the sausages back in. Bring the pan to a boil then reduce to a simmer and cook uncovered for around 15-20 minutes or until the sausages are cooked through and the apples are just tender.

INGREDIENTS

4 Chicken Thighs, bone in
Splash of Oil
1 Onion, finely chopped
2 Celery Stalks, finely chopped
2 Carrots, diced into small cubes
2 Garlic Cloves, finely chopped
1 heaped tbsp Flour
1 glass of White Wine
1 Chicken Stock Cube
1 tsp Thyme
½ tsp Celery Salt (optional)
50g Frozen Peas
Splash of Cream

A few serving ideas to try:

(1) Place it in a casserole dish and top with mashed potatoes before baking in the oven.

(2) Add a pastry topping to make a more traditional pot pie.

(3) It also tastes really good just served up as it is, over a bed of rice.

Chicken Pot Pie Filling

Serves 4

This is so versatile you can do lots of recipes with it. Just use it as a base and go for whatever takes your fancy on the day. It freezes really well so why not double up and put a portion in the freezer for one of those nights you are feeling too lazy to cook. If you don't want to use a slow cooker this can easily be made on the hob.

INSTRUCTIONS

Add the oil, onions, celery, and carrots to a slow cooker and fry for about 5 minutes. Add the garlic and continue frying for a few more minutes. Add in the flour and give it a mix. Stir in the wine to deglaze the bottom of the pan.

Now add in the chicken thighs along with a pint of water, the chicken stock cube, thyme and celery salt. Stir together then bring to the boil. Put the lid on and cook on slow cooker mode for 4 hours.

Just before it is ready take out the chicken. Once able to handle, remove the meat off the bone, shred and return to the pot. Add in the peas and cream and give it a final stir.

Once warmed through the pot pie base is now ready.

Burgers

All recipes serves 4 (you will need 4 burger buns for each recipe)

Who doesn't love a burger? Well if we are talking beef burgers then the answer is me. I much prefer something lighter with a bit more flavour. I made up the mushroom burger below when I was thinking of new ideas to feed my brother Paul as he is a vegetarian and I am always thinking of recipes to make using fresh ingredients that are not a soy based product imitating real meat! Even non veggies will enjoy it.

INSTRUCTIONS

Mushroom, Leek and Blue Cheese Burgers

Crush 2 garlic cloves into a small bowl, squeeze in the juice of a lemon and add a good pinch of salt and lots of cracked black pepper. Give it a good mix and then spoon evenly over 4 Portobello mushrooms.

Leave to marinate for about 30 minutes. When it is time to cook the burger simply add a splash of oil to a frying pan and fry the whole mushrooms on a medium heat for around 5 minutes each side.

Meanwhile chop up two leeks and gently fry them in a knob of butter until soft.

To assemble the burgers add the mushrooms to the buns, then some blue cheese and a final layer of the leeks.

You can use any blue cheese for this recipe or if you do not like blue cheese then simply replace with a cheese of choice. Feta would also work well with this burger.

Thai Pork Burgers

Add 1lb pork mince to a bowl. Very finely dice a small onion. Grate a thumb sized piece of ginger. Crush 2 garlic cloves and now add them all to the mince.

Add a tablespoon each on cumin and coriander then a heaped tablespoon of Thai curry paste. Add a pinch of salt and pepper. Give it a good mix and divide into 4 equal sized burgers.

You can prepare the burgers either on the hob, under the grill, in the oven or even on the BBQ.

Whichever method you choose just cook the burgers using a medium heat until the pork is cooked all the way through.

You can eat these burgers simply on their own or you can top with the quick tasty pineapple salsa (recipe shown).

Burgers

All recipes serves 4 (you will need 4 burger buns for each recipe)

INSTRUCTIONS

Spicy Chicken and Pineapple Burger

Mix together 1 tablespoon of each, Cajun spice, paprika and garlic salt.

Use 4 medium sized chicken breasts and flatten them out with a rolling pin if too thick. Then cover with the spice rub.

Place a drizzle of oil into a frying pan and cook the chicken on a medium heat for about 5 minutes each side or until they are cooked all the way through.

Serve on a bun with iceberg lettuce, a slice of avocado (optional) and a tablespoon of the pineapple salsa (recipe shown).

You can change up the rub here to any flavour combination you like. Try mixing together cumin, coriander, paprika and garlic salt. Even a shop bought rub would work well.

Crispy Fish Burger

Mix together 4 tablespoons of Panko breadcrumbs along with 1 tablespoon of sesame seeds and place in a shallow dish.

Take 4 fish fillets (most white fish work well) and lightly coat them with a thin layer of mayonnaise. Make sure you do not put too much mayonnaise on the fish or the flavour will over power the burger.

Now press the fish down into the breadcrumb mixture and cover both sides. Put a drizzle of oil in a frying pan and cook the fish for approximately 2-3 minutes each side. The exact timings will depend on what fish you are using and how thick it is.

Serve on the bun with crispy lettuce and tartar sauce.

If you want to make your own tartar sauce mix together mayonnaise, finely chopped capers and gherkins, chopped parsley and a squeeze of lemon juice.

Pineapple Salsa

To make the salsa simply mix together chopped pineapple (tinned or fresh), sliced spring onions, a squeeze of lime juice and some chopped coriander. Add in some finely chopped chilli if you want to add some additional heat (I normally do!).

INGREDIENTS

For the Base Filling
Splash of Olive Oil
1 ½ lb lean Lamb, cubed
1 large Onion, finely chopped
3 Garlic Cloves, finely chopped
1 large thumb-sized piece of
Ginger, finely chopped
10 Cardamom Pods, seeds removed
1tbsp of each Cumin and Coriander
1 Red Chilli chopped (add more or
 less depending on heat preference)
2 tbsp Tomato Puree
1 pint of Chicken Stock
14oz tin of Coconut Milk
10 fresh Curry Leaves
1 Aubergine, cubed
200g of Spinach, chopped (optional)

For the Potato Topping
4 large Potatoes
1 tsp Turmeric
2 tsp Cumin Seeds
10 fresh Curry Leaves
Pinch of Salt

> **NOTE**
> You can substitute stewing beef for the
> lamb in this recipe and it is still really
> yum. Cooking times may change
> though so just cook until the meat is
> soft. You could also use chicken but I
> think red meat works best.

Curried Lamb Casserole

Serves 4

This is a fairly easy dish to make and is great for when you have people coming over to dinner as it can be made well in advance. It also makes a relatively inexpensive meal as you can bulk it out by adding potatoes and extra side portions to the dish. It looks quite impressive in the middle of the table too.

INSTRUCTIONS

Heat Oven to 400°F / 200 °C / Gas Mark 6

Add the oil to a pan then add in the lamb, onion, garlic and ginger. Fry until the onions start to soften a little. Add in the cardamom, cumin and coriander and cook for a few minutes more. Now add the chilli, tomato puree, chicken stock, coconut milk and curry leaves and give it a good stir.

Cover and simmer for about an hour or until the meat begins to soften and the sauce reduces a little. At this stage add the aubergine and spinach and cook for about another 30 minutes or until both the lamb and vegetables are super tender and the sauce is a nice thick curry like texture. Add extra water along the way if needed.

While that is cooking prepare the topping by peeling the potatoes and cutting them into large cubes. Boil the potatoes for about 10-15 minutes or until they are just starting to go soft but still firm. When ready drain and then toss with the turmeric, cumin seeds, the curry leaves and salt.

Once the base filling and the potato topping are ready simply spread the lamb filling evenly into a casserole dish and top with the potato mixture. Bake in the oven for about an hour or until the base is bubbling and the potatoes are nicely brown.

I like to serve this with naan bread or an Indian type salad (try sliced red onion, sliced tomatoes, cucumber and coriander) or my favourite is a side portion of Spicy Green Beans (the naan and green beans recipes are shown in my 'Sides" section).

INGREDIENTS

1lb Beef Mince
1 Onion, finely chopped
1 Red Pepper, diced
2 Garlic Cloves, finely chopped
1 tbsp Cumin and Coriander
½ tbsp Paprika and Garlic Salt
1 tsp Chilli Powder (add more or less depending on heat preferences)
1 Beef Stock Cube
400g tin Chopped Tomatoes
425g tin Red Kidney Beans or Black Beans
Pinch of Salt and Pepper

☑ Veg Option – you could switch out the mince for cooked green (puy) lentils or add in a few vegetables like butternut squash or cubed aubergine pieces.

NOTE
For a more indulgent chilli why not try substituting the beef mince with stewing steak. You will just need to cook for about an hour longer as the meat will take longer to soften.

I serve this over rice and my kids like grated cheddar over the top – scrummyness on a plate. To change it up, Adam sometimes has his chilli with pasta. All you need to do is cook your pasta according to the instructions, drain then mix in the chilli and a big handful of grated cheddar. Sounds a bit odd but he seems to like it anyways!!

Chilli Con Carne

Serves 4

This is a great recipe to double and freeze. I like to freeze them in individual portions so if I am stuck for what to feed the kids on an occasion when we are having a meal they don't particularly like, it is so easy just to take them out of the freezer and re-heat in the microwave. Anything which saves time and hassle has to be good!

INSTRUCTIONS

Add the beef mince to the pan and sauté until it turns brown all over. Drain off any excess fat then add the onions, red pepper and garlic and stir until they soften. Now add the cumin, coriander, paprika, garlic salt, chilli powder, salt and pepper. Add the tin of chopped tomatoes along with one and a half tins of water and the beef stock cube. Stir while bringing to the boil, then reduce the heat down to a simmer and continue to cook for approximately 30 minutes.

Drain and rinse the beans thoroughly then add the beans into the chilli and continue to cook for about another 10 minutes or until the beef and onions are completely soft and the sauce has reduced to a thick consistency. If more water is needed just top up as you go.

INGREDIENTS

Splash of Olive Oil
1 Onion, finely chopped
2 Garlic Cloves, finely chopped
½ Red Chilli, chopped (add more or less depending on heat preference)
4 Roma Tomatoes, chopped
Splash of White Wine
2 tbsp Black Olives, chopped
2 large handfuls of Rocket
Large handful of Cherry Tomatoes, sliced in half
2 small Fillet Steaks, finely sliced
Squeeze of Lemon (optional)
4 tbsp crumbled Feta Cheese
400g of Pasta (Spaghetti or Tagliatelle are good choices)

 Veg Option

Why not switch out the meat for sliced mushrooms or cubed aubergine?

Steak Pasta

Serves 4

I had a version of this once in an Italian restaurant a million years ago. It was delicious so I decided to try and recreate it at home. This is what I came up with and I have been making it ever since.

INSTRUCTIONS

Start by cooking your pasta according to the packet instructions, which takes normally between 10-15 minutes, or to the texture your like your pasta.

While the pasta is cooking add the oil to a pan and sauté the onions for about 5 minutes until they soften. Then add the garlic and chilli and fry for a few more minutes. Now add the Roma tomatoes and wine and cook until the tomatoes become mushy and broken down into a sauce.

Once the onion and tomato mixture is ready add the olives, rocket, cherry tomatoes and the steak. Cook for a further couple of minutes to wilt the rocket, warm the olives and tomatoes and cook the steak. I like my steak medium rare so with the thin slices this will only take a couple of minutes maximum.

Drain the pasta and add it to the mixture. Stir in a squeeze of lemon juice (if using) and salt and pepper if needed. Finish off by adding the feta and giving it a quick stir before serving.

INGREDIENTS

1 lb Beef Mince
1 lb Pork Mince or Sausage Meat
1 Onion, finely chopped
2 tbsp flavoured Breadcrumbs
1 heaped tbsp Tomato Ketchup
1 heaped tbsp Mayonnaise
Pinch of Salt and Pepper

I like to serve my meatloaf with mashed potato (with wholegrain mustard stirred through for me), broccoli and mashed carrot and parsnip but it goes well with any vegetables. You can make it more decadent by serving with dauphinoise potatoes if you dare!!

Mommas Meatloaf

Serves 4

My lovely Mummy used to make this recipe for me when I was growing up and now I make it for my family. Everyone loves it except Lauren but she doesn't eat much red meat anyways. It is so quick to make and is always juicy. A hit in our house every time.

INSTRUCTIONS

Heat Oven to 400°F / 200 °C / Gas Mark 6
Use a 23 x 14 x 8cm Loaf Tin

Simply add all the ingredients to a bowl and mix. Try not to over mix as it will tend to make the meatloaf dense.

Once mixed place in a loaf tin and press down. Cook in the oven for around 25-30 minutes or until cooked through. I tend to drain the fat off into an old tin or into a bowl halfway through cooking.

When ready take it out of the oven, drain the fat again then cover with an oven glove or a clean tea towel and let it rest for just a couple of minutes before serving.

INGREDIENTS

2 lb Beef Mince
2 Onions, finely chopped
4 large Carrots, diced into small cubes
3 tbsp Tomato Puree
2 Beef Stock Cubes
2-3 tbsp Gravy Granules
Mash Potato (enough to top your pie)
Grated Cheese for topping (optional)

Shepherd's Pie with Love

Serves 4-6

The reason this is made with love is that it's not actually something I enjoy eating very much. However, Andy and the kids all love it!! That is why it is made with love as I make it for them and make myself something else!! It is one of the household favourites (for them anyways). We have actually been known to have this instead of Turkey on Christmas Day on more than a couple of occasions.

INSTRUCTIONS

Heat Oven to 400°F / 200 °C / Gas Mark 6

Fry the mince until brown all over then drain off any excess fat. Now add the onions and carrots and stir until the onions just start to soften. Add your tomato puree and stir until thoroughly mixed.

Add about a pint of water and the stock cube and bring to the boil then reduce to a simmer. Cook for around 30 minutes or until the mixture has reduced quite significantly and the vegetables are soft. Do not reduce down too much as the next stage will be adding the gravy granules which will over thicken the filling if you have reduced too much. Top up with extra water as you go if needed.

To finish off add the gravy granules and stir for just a minute until it is all incorporated and the mixture goes nice and gloopy.

Place the mince mixture evenly in a casserole dish and cover with the mashed potato. Depending on whether you have made it in advance or have just prepared this now will depend on how long it will take to cook. If cooking while still warm it should only take about 20-25 minutes but if made in advance and cooked from room temperature it will probably take around 40-45 minutes. Either way, ensure that it is bubbling hot all the way through and the mash has started to brown.

You can also add grated cheese to this before baking but we have a divide in our house. Lauren no cheese, boys cheese, so I sometimes end up doing separate dishes. The boys also like serving this with cold baked beans (what?? I hear you say – I know right - gross!!) – Oh my days!!

INGREDIENTS

Meat Sauce

1 ½ lb Beef Mince
1 Onion, finely chopped
225g Mushrooms, sliced
2 Garlic Cloves, finely chopped
1 tbsp Tomato Puree
400g tin Chopped Tomatoes
1 Beef Stock Cube
1 tbsp of both Italian Herbs and Oregano
2 tsps Garlic Powder (optional)
Pinch of Salt and Pepper
1-2 tbsp Beef Gravy Granules (optional)

Cheese Sauce

2 tbsp Margarine or Butter
2 ½ tbsp Plain Flour
400 ml Milk (any type)
125g Cheddar Cheese, grated
8 Lasagne Sheets (or enough for 4 layers depending on size)

> **NOTE**
> The meat sauce is exactly the same as I would make it when making a spaghetti bolognaise. Why not double the ingredients and freeze half for an easy mid-week supper. All you need to do is boil some pasta up, reheat the sauce and then sprinkle with parmesan cheese.

We serve this with a light garden salad made up of lettuce, tomatoes and onion along with yummy garlic bread. My father in law likes a well-known brand of brown sauce squidged on the side (much to the disgust of my mother in law!!) For me it a dollop of mayo on my salad, for Andy it is that very famous yellow salad dressing squirted all over his. Each to their own I suppose.

Lasagne

Serves 4

This is one of everyone's favourite dinners in our family including my Mum. Well except for Lauren but even she has learnt to like it (minus the chunks of mushrooms).

INSTRUCTIONS

Heat Oven to 400°F / 200 °C / Gas Mark 6
Use a casserole dish approximately 8x8"

Add the beef mince to the pan and sauté until it turns brown all over. Drain off any excess fat then add the onions, mushrooms and garlic and stir until they soften. At this stage add the tomato puree and mix until well combined. Add the tin of chopped tomatoes along with one and a half tins of water, the stock cube, Italian herbs, oregano, garlic powder, salt and pepper and stir.

Bring to the boil then reduce the heat down to a simmer and continue to cook for approximately 30 minutes or until the beef, onions and mushrooms have cooked and the sauce has reduced to a thick consistency. If more water is needed just top up as you go. When nearly ready I like to add one to two tablespoons of gravy granules to thicken the sauce up and give it a more meaty finish.

While the mince mixture is cooling slightly start on your cheese sauce. Add the margarine (or butter if using), the milk and the flour to a pan. Start cooking on a medium heat, whisking all the time until it becomes a nice, thick white sauce. Lower the heat and add in the cheese until it has melted.

Once the sauce is ready you can start layering. I like to start with a very thin layer of mince first just so the pasta doesn't stick to the bottom of the dish. So it is mince sauce followed by a lasagne sheet, followed by a thin layer of cheese sauce. Repeat 4 times until you have the last layer of pasta on the top. Now cover with the remaining cheese sauce. You can add extra grated cheese on top if you like.

Cook in the oven for 30 minutes or until it is fully cooked through and bubbling up the sides with the top starting go a lovely golden brown (this may take longer if you have made the lasagne in advance and it is cold when putting in the oven).

Once cooked take it out of the oven and leave for about 5 minutes under a clean tea towel to let it "set".

INGREDIENTS

For the Meatballs
1 lb Beef Mince
1 lb Pork Mince
1 Onion, very finely chopped
3 tbsp Parmesan Cheese
1 Garlic Clove, finely chopped
1 heaped tsp of Dried Mint
Pinch of Salt and Pepper

For the Tomato Sauce
Splash of Olive Oil
1 Onion, finely chopped
2 Garlic Clove, finely chopped
1 Red Pepper, finely chopped
1 tbsp Tomato Puree
400g tin Chopped Tomatoes
Splash of White or Red Wine
1 tbsp Oregano
1 tsp Italian Herbs
Pinch of Salt, Pepper and Sugar
Pinch Chilli Flakes (add more or less
depending on heat preference)
Handful of fresh Basil
Sprinkle of Parmesan to serve

> NOTE
> If you are not using a mixture of both
> pork and beef mince and are just using
> beef then first start the meatballs by
> soaking a piece of white bread in milk
> then mush it all up like breadcrumbs.
> Mix this into the beef mixture as it will
> help keep the meatballs moist.

*I prefer spaghetti with this dish but
everyone has their own preference. Adam
likes pasta full stop so he doesn't care
what it comes with as long as it's pasta!!
But it's totally up to you!!!*

My Meatballs

Serves 4 people, with possible leftover portions for freezing

I love meatballs. It's my favourite thing to eat. As I use both beef mince and pork mince I tend to make too many meatballs for just one sitting so once I have cooked them (in stage 2), I let them cool and I freeze a portion in a freezer bag or container. They are then ready just to defrost when needed and all you have to do is make another sauce, add the meatballs and warm through.

INSTRUCTIONS

Heat Oven to 400°F / 200 °C / Gas Mark 6

Firstly make the meatballs by adding the beef and pork mince to a bowl along with the chopped onions, garlic, dried mint, parmesan, salt and pepper (and the soaked bread if not using the pork mince).

Mix gently until all the ingredients are combined. Try not to over mix as this will make the meatballs less moist. Then roll into small bite size balls and place on a tray which has been covered in tin foil. Bake in the oven for approximately 10-15 minutes or until they start to brown slightly. When ready take them out and just leave to cool.

While the meatballs are cooling start on the sauce. Add the oil to a pan and fry the onions and peppers on a medium heat for approximately 10 minutes or until softened. Then add the tomato puree and garlic and cook for another couple of minutes.

Add the chopped tomatoes, wine, oregano, Italian herbs, chilli flakes, salt, pepper and sugar. Add a tin of water, stir and then bring to the boil. Once boiling reduce to a simmer and cook for approximately 15-20 minutes or until the vegetables are soft and the sauce becomes thick enough to coat the pasta nicely.

Once the sauce is nearly ready add the meatballs back in along with the fresh basil and cook for a further 10 minutes. Once ready you can mix with the pasta of your choice.

Either mix together in the pan or put the pasta in a bowl and top with the meatballs and sauce and sprinkle over the parmesan.

INGREDIENTS

1 ½ lb lean Lamb or Beef, cubed
1 large Onion, quartered
3 Garlic Cloves
2 small thumb sized pieces of Ginger
1 tbsp of each Cumin and Coriander
1 tsp Tumeric
½ tsp Fennel Seeds
4 Cardamom Seeds, de-podded
1 Cinnamon Stick
1 Red or Green Chilli, chopped
(add more or less depending on heat preference)
2 tbsp Desiccated Coconut
1 Chicken Stock Cube
400g tin Chopped Tomatoes
3 tbsp Coriander Stalks, finely chopped
Pinch of Salt and Pepper

This eats well with basmati rice and my favourite side portion of Spicy Green Beans (as per recipe shown in my "Sides" section). You can also add a cheeky portion of naan bread. This freezes really well so if you have made too much just portion up and bang in the freezer for an easy Friday night dinner.

Cardamom Meat Curry

Serves 4

Simple to prepare but so authentic you might think it came from the Indian Take Away but nicer! I cook this in the slow cooker so I can just add in all the ingredients and leave it to do its magic. You can do it in a pan on the hob, you will just have to keep stirring it.

INSTRUCTIONS

Add the onion, garlic and half the ginger to a food processor and blitz to a puree. Add to the slow cooker and fry until all the excess liquid has disappeared.

Slice the remaining ginger into thin strips and add that to the slow cooker along with the chilli, all the spices and the meat and stir for a further 5 minutes. Once the meat changes colour add the tomatoes, desiccated coconut, chicken stock cube, coriander stalks, salt and pepper. Give it a good stir.

Bring the curry to the boil and leave to cook for 4 hours. If cooking on the hob cover and simmer for about an hour or until the meat has soften and the sauce reduces to a loose curry like consistence. Add water at any time during cooking if the sauce becomes too dry.

INGREDIENTS

4 x oversized, frozen Yorkshire Puddings
1 Onion, finely chopped
3 Carrots, cubed
Small glass of White Wine
1 Beef Stock Cube
2 Potatoes, cubed
2 x 392g tins of Stewed Steak in gravy
Handful of frozen Sprouts
Handful of frozen Sweetcorn
Handful of frozen Peas
2 tbsp of Gravy Granules
2 tsp Mint Sauce (optional)

You could make homemade Yorkshire puddings but it will take longer. In this recipe I mixed together 4 eggs, 1 cup of flour, ¾ cup of milk and a pinch of salt, which I cooked in 4 round baking tins 8inch x 8inch. You could also use fresh stewing steak but the cooking times will take much longer and you will definitely need to add gravy granules at the end of cooking to achieve the thick sauce needed for this recipe.

Casserole Stuffed Yorkshires

Serves 4

If you are looking for a quick and easy Sunday roast substitute this recipe is for you. You can change up the vegetables by just throwing in any you have to hand. It is a great way of using up those sad left over veggies in the bottom draw of the fridge.

INSTRUCTIONS

Heat oven as per packet instructions for Yorkshires

Add the onions and carrots to a large pan and cover with 1 ½ pints of water. Bring to the boil then add the white wine and stock cube. Reduce to a simmer and cook for about 10 minutes. Now add in the potatoes and cook for a further 10 minutes until all the vegetables are tender and the liquid has evaporated by about half.

While the vegetables are cooking check the cooking time needed for the Yorkshire puddings and put them in to reheat so they are cooked for when the casserole is ready. Once the vegetables are nearly tender add the tinned stewing steak, sprouts, sweetcorn and peas and stir until combined. Cook for a further 5-10 minutes or until heated all the way through and the sprouts are cooked to your liking (everyone likes them differently by my experience).

Now stir the gravy granules and mint sauce (if using) into the casserole then serve up. You can leave out the mint sauce but I think it just adds that little extra flavour and zing.

INGREDIENTS

1lb Beef Mince
1 Onion, finely chopped
2 Garlic Cloves, finely chopped
1 tbsp Cumin
1 tbsp Coriander
1 tbsp Curry Powder
1 tbsp Tomato Puree
1 Beef Stock Cube
180g Frozen Peas

As with most curries I like to serve this with a portion of basmati rice. When I was growing up we were served slices of fresh tomato, sliced cucumbers and onions on the side of a curry. I think it was to cool the palate but that is definitely not required here. However, you could easily spice it up by adding more chilli.

Intro Curry

Serves 4

I call this Intro Curry as it was Lauren and Adams first introduction to a curry. It is a lot milder than a full on curry but full of flavour without being too over powering, especially for the younger pallet. It also has very few ingredients.

INSTRUCTIONS

Fry the mince in a pan until brown all over then drain off any excess fat. Add in the onions and garlic and continue to cook for about 10 more minutes until the onions start to soften.

Add the cumin, coriander and curry powder and stir around for another minute. Add in the tomato puree and cook for a further minute. Now add a pint of water and the beef stock cube. Bring to the boil then reduce to a simmer. Continue to cook for around 15-20 minutes or until the mince is totally soft and the sauce has reduced down to a curry like consistency. Add extra water as you go should you need it. Finish off by adding the peas and warming them through before serving.

INGREDIENTS

1 425g Tin of Beans
1 Thumb sized piece of Ginger
5 Garlic Cloves
½ Red Onion, finely chopped
200g Cherry Tomatoes
2 Dried Chillis
1 Jalapeno, sliced down the length
½ tbsp Tomato Puree
1 tsp Cumin and Coriander Seeds
½ tsp Smoked Paprika
¼ tsp Tumeric and Chilli Powder
1 tbsp Olive Oil
Pinch of Salt

To Top
90g Greek Plain Yoghurt
1 small Garlic Clove
Small handful of Mint
Small handful Coriander
Juice of ½ Lime

*For me the beans are quite filling so I
would normally just eat this on its own
but if I were feeding the boys or guests
I would add a portion of rice and naan
bread to bulk the dish out a little. As with
my non vegetarian curries my side
portion of spicy green beans would work
a treat here too (recipe shown in my
"Sides section")*

Baked Tandoori Beans

Serves 2

You can use any type of beans in this recipe. Chickpeas or butter beans would work really well but I prefer something like a cannellini bean which I have used here.

INSTRUCTIONS

Heat Oven to 350°F / 170 °C / Gas Mark 3

Drain the beans and give them a rinse in a colander. Cut the ginger in half then grate one half and finely julienne the other. Crush one of the garlic cloves then cut the remaining cloves in half.

Now add the beans, ginger and garlic to an oven proof casserole dish that has a lid. Add all the remaining ingredients along with a tablespoon of water and give it a stir. Cover with the lid and bake in the oven for 60 minutes, giving it a good stir half way through cooking. Remove the lid after an hour and continue to cook for a further 15 minutes. Discard the chillies before serving especially if you do not like your food too spicy.

Place the yoghurt, garlic, mint, coriander and lime into a food processor and blitz until smooth. Set aside until the beans are cooked. Once ready simply serve the beans up with a dollop of the yoghurt dressing on top.

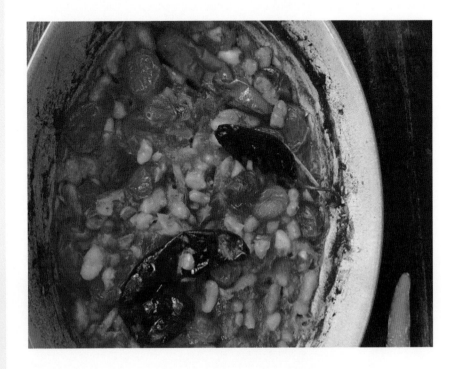

INGREDIENTS

For the Cheese Sauce

2 tbsp Margarine or Butter
2 ½ tbsp Plain Flour
400 ml of Milk (any type)
125g grated Cheddar Cheese

Cheesy Pasta in So Many Ways

Serves 4

I couldn't do a recipe book without cheesy pasta. It is a weekly staple in our house and the person who enjoys it the most is Adam. Over the years I have tried a number of versions using different ingredients to change up the recipe.

INSTRUCTIONS

If baking - Heat Oven to 400°F / 200 °C / Gas Mark 6

Firstly choose what pasta you would like to use and put enough to serve 4 people into a pan and on to boil.

You are supposed to cook your pasta El Dente but we like ours over cooked if that is the case. It normally takes around 10-15 minutes to cook depending which pasta you are using.

Once the pasta is on start making the cheese sauce base. Add the butter to a pan and melt. Once melted add in the flour and cook gently for a couple of minutes so the flour cooks out.

Now you need to add the milk in very slowly, bit by bit, as you continue to whisk. If you add the milk too quickly you will end up with lots of lumps which does not taste good.

Once you have a thick white sauce add your cheese and stir until well mixed. Now add your drained pasta and voila you have your pasta meal base.

There are a number of different variations – try any of these below.

Plain Mac n Cheese
Try adding extra indulgence like mascarpone, parmesan, blue cheese or any combination of cheeses to the cheese sauce before you mix with the pasta.

Tuna Pasta
After combining the cheese sauce with the pasta add in a tin of tuna and 150g defrosted frozen sweetcorn (or you could use tinned sweetcorn if you prefer).

Bacon and Pea
After combining the cheese sauce with the pasta add in 50g bacon bits (or fry up a small packet of pancetta) and 150g defrosted frozen peas.

Chicken and Broccoli
After combining the cheese sauce with the pasta add in 500g of cooked chicken (either shredded or diced) and 150g steamed broccoli florets.

Mushroom, Pea and Bacon
After combining the cheese sauce with the pasta add in 2 tablespoon of rehydrated and finely chopped porcini mushrooms along with a touch of the soaking liquid, 150g defrosted frozen peas and 50g of bacon bits (or fry up a small packet of pancetta).

To be honest the combinations are limitless. Just make your base and add in any ingredient you like. It's pasta – whatever you add it will be delicious!!

INGREDIENTS

Splash of Olive Oil
20g Dried Porcini Mushrooms
1 Onion, quartered
2 Garlic Cloves
1 stalk of Celery, halved
1 Carrot, quartered
225g Mushrooms (any type)
1 tbsp Tomato Puree
400g Tin of Chopped Tomatoes
1 small glass of Red Wine
1 tbsp Italian Herbs
1 tbsp Oregano
2 tsp Garlic Powder
Pinch of Salt and Pepper
400g of Pasta of choice
2 tbsp Parmesan Cheese, grated

You could add chilli flakes to this recipe if you prefer a bit more heat. If you are not vegetarian and are trying to cut out meat to be a bit healthier then you could also add in a beef stock cube or some beef gravy granules which will add another level of meatiness.

Mushroom Bolognaise

Serves 4

The porcini mushrooms and their liquid really add an extra level of richness and meaty flavour to this dish. The chopped mushrooms and vegetables really change the texture of the bolognaise too without having to use a meat replacement. Go on give it a go I think you will be pleasantly surprised at how good it actually tastes.

INSTRUCTIONS

Put the porcini mushrooms in a bowl or large mug and cover ½ of the way up with boiling water. Leave for a minimum of 30 minutes to let the mushrooms re-hydrate.

Add half the fresh mushrooms, the onion, garlic, celery and carrot to a food processor and finely chop. Once all chopped up add them to a pan along with the olive oil. Slice the remaining mushrooms and add them to the pan as well then cook on a medium heat for around 10 minutes until the vegetables have softened. Add in the tomato puree and give it a stir. Take the porcini mushrooms out of the water, squeeze and reserve the liquid. Chop the mushrooms up finely and add them to the pan along with the reserved soaking liquid (be careful not to get the gritty bits at the bottom).

Next add in the tomatoes and fill up the empty can half way up with water and add that too. Now add in the red wine, Italian herbs, oregano, garlic salt and a pinch of salt and pepper. Bring to the boil then reduce the heat down to a simmer and cook uncovered for around 25-30 minutes or until all the vegetables are completely soft and the sauce has reduced down to a medium thick consistency. Mix with your pasta of choice and serve up with a sprinkling of parmesan cheese.

INGREDIENTS

Splash of Olive Oil
1 Onion, finely chopped
1 Red Pepper, diced
2 Celery Sticks, finely chopped
2 Garlic Cloves, finely chopped
1 tsp each Cumin and Coriander
1 tsp each Chilli and Paprika
½ tsp Thyme
1 tbsp Tomato Puree
250g fresh Tomatoes, chopped
(around 1 punnet of cherry tomatoes)
400g of Vegetable Stock
2 Carrots, cubed
2 Parsnips, cubed
1 large Potato, cubed

You can change up the veggies by adding anything you have left over in the bottom of your fridge. Try butternut squash or sweet potato. Why not add some shredded kale in the last five minutes of cooking to add another level of flavour.

Veggie Stew

Serves 4

This is such a lovely and appetising bowl of goodness that you won't even notice you have gone vegetarian. You can serve this on its own but for those with a bigger appetite serve over a bed of rice or even add a tin of beans to the recipe.

INSTRUCTIONS

Make sure all your vegetables such as carrots, parsnips, potato etc. are cut into similar sizes so they cook at the same time (medium chunks work well).

Add the oil, onions, red pepper and celery to a pan and sauté on a medium heat for around 5-10 minutes or until softened a little. Add in the garlic and all the spices and give it stir. Add the tomato puree and stir again. Now add the chopped tomatoes, stock, carrots, parsnip and the potato and mix well.

Bring to the boil then reduce to a simmer and cook for around 20 minutes or until the vegetables are tender and the liquid has evaporated by half. If more liquid is required just top up with a bit of water.

Taste, then add salt and pepper if required. Serve in a bowl.

INGREDIENTS

2 tbsp Olive Oil
1 Preserved Lemon
2 Garlic Cloves, finely chopped
1 tbsp Coriander Seeds, crushed
½ tbsp Tomato Puree
½ Red Chilli, finely diced
2 Rosemary Sprigs, left whole
½ tbsp fresh Thyme Leaves, chopped
1 425g Tin of Beans
1 large Tomato
Pinch of Salt and Pepper

I like to serve this with a green side salad as it adds a freshness to the dish and as always a big chunk of crusty bread wouldn't go a miss either to help mop up the juices. It would also work great as part of a tapas.

Beans with Preserved Lemon and Spice

Serves 2

You can use any type of beans in this recipe. A white bean such as butter bean would work perfectly as they absorb all the flavours really well. But just choose your favourite and go with that.

INSTRUCTIONS

Heat Oven to 350°F / 170 °C / Gas Mark 3

Cut the preserved lemon in half and discard the inside fleshy part. Finely slice the skin then add to a frying pan along with the olive oil, garlic, coriander seeds, tomato puree, chilli, rosemary and thyme. Add a splash of water and a pinch of salt and pepper. Cook on a very low heat for about 15 minutes.

Stir in the beans and cook for a further 10 minutes then remove from the heat and leave to cool while all the flavour infuse. Try and leave for at least an hour.

Meanwhile grate the tomato on a box grater discarding the skins. Mix in a pinch of salt and pepper and stir. When the beans are ready mix in the grated tomato and serve.

INGREDIENTS

Tomatoes
1 large Beef Tomato
2 tbsp Couscous
2 tbsp boiling Water
½ Chicken Stock Cube
1 tsp Oregano

Tzatziki
75g Plain unsweetened Yoghurt (½ a pot)
1 inch piece of Cucumber
1 Garlic Clove, crushed
½ tsp Olive Oil
Pinch of Salt and Pepper
Pinch of Cayenne (optional)

Roast Vegetables
Vegetables of Choice
Splash of Olive Oil
1 tsp Oregano, Rosemary and Garlic Salt
1 tbsp of Feta Cheese (optional)
Pinch of Salt and Pepper

NOTE
For the roast vegetables in this recipe I used ½ courgette, ¼ onion, 6 cherry tomatoes, 4 mini red peppers and 1 clove of garlic. But you can add whatever vegetables you have lying around.

Stuffed Greek Tomatoes

Serves 1 – just me!

This recipe serves 1 person as I am the only one in our house that enjoys it which I cannot understand as I love it!! I worked in Greece during the summer of 1992 and we have been on lots of Greek holidays over the years and one of my favourite things about being in Greece is eating the Greek food. This recipe reminds me of great times spent chilling on holidays with family and friends.

INSTRUCTIONS

Heat Oven to 400°F / 200 °C / Gas Mark 6

Prepare your tzatziki by grating the cucumber then squeezing out the excess water in your hands. Add the cucumber to a bowl and mix it with the yoghurt, garlic, olive oil, salt, pepper and cayenne if using. Give it a really good stir then leave it in the fridge until you are ready to serve.

Put the couscous into a bowl. Sprinkle in the oregano and chicken stock cube then pour over 2 tablespoons of boiling water and cover. Leave to absorb the water while you prepare the rest of the tomato. Cut the top part of the tomato off about 2cm down. Scoop out the inside, remove the hard middle part, then chop the remaining flesh up finely. Add the tomato flesh to the couscous and give it a good stir. Fill the tomato with the couscous pushing it in as tightly as possible. Put the tomato top back on and cover tightly in tin foil.

Now simply prepare your vegetables by placing whatever you have chosen to use into a casserole dish and sprinkling on the oregano, garlic salt, rosemary, salt and pepper. Give it a splash of oil and a good mix. You can now place the tomato and vegetables in the oven for about 40-45 minutes or until cooked. When ready finish the vegetables off by adding the feta and serve them both with a side portion of tzatziki.

If you fancied a non-vegetarian meal why not substitute the stuffed tomato with marinated chicken (legs, thighs or breast would all work well). I have had that at many a BBQ!

INGREDIENTS

1 large head of Broccoli
Splash of Olive Oil
1 tsp Garlic Salt
1 tsp Chilli Flakes
A squeeze of Lemon Juice
Pinch of Salt and Pepper

Roasted Broccoli

Serves 4

I love broccoli but just steaming it sometimes get a bit boring. By roasting the broccoli it gives it a really different flavour. You could try roasting carrots or parsnips too (they are great par boiled then roasted in honey).

INSTRUCTIONS

Cut the broccoli into bite size florets and wash. Spread them over a baking tray or in a casserole dish and sprinkle over the olive oil, garlic salt and chilli flakes. Give them a good stir to coat evenly then bake in the oven (oven at 400°F / 200 °C / Gas Mark 6) for about 15-20 minutes until softened and just starting to brown up. Take out of the oven and squeeze over the lemon juice and sprinkle with salt and pepper.

INGREDIENTS

4 jacket sized Potatoes (or enough to feed 4 people)
2 tbsp Ranch Dressing (Mayonnaise can be substituted)
1 tbsp of each Garlic Salt and Paprika
30g Bacon Bits (or a small pack of Pancetta fried until golden)
125g grated Cheddar Cheese
Salt and Pepper

Cheesy Bacon Spuds

Serves 4

This doesn't take too long to prepare and it can be made in advance. I like to serve it as an accompaniment with a BBQ as it goes great with grilled chicken, ribs or even a burger. I use a throw away tin when hosting so less washing up afterwards. It can also be easily doubled if you are serving a crowd. For a tasty vegetarian option just leave out the bacon.

INSTRUCTIONS

Peel your potatoes and cut them into 2cm diced cubes. Par boil for around 5-10 minutes or until just starting to soften. Once ready drain them and add back into the pan.

Add in all the other ingredients, give it a good stir and transfer into an oven proof dish or tin.

You can cook straight away (oven at 400°F / 200 °C / Gas Mark 6) which will take about 15-20 minutes or re-heat at a later time which will take slightly longer at 25-30 minutes.

INGREDIENTS

1 lb Brussel Sprouts (or enough
to feed 4 people)
1 large Garlic Clove, crushed
1 Chicken Stock Cube
A pinch of Thyme
1 tbsp Butter
Pinch of Salt and Pepper
Squeeze of Lemon Juice (optional).

Yummy Brussel Sprouts

Serves 4

I promise you if you like brussels you will love this recipe. It is so simple yet so very tasty. You may even be converted if you are not a fan of the sprout. Go on give it a try!

INSTRUCTIONS

Remove any dirty outer layers of the spouts then cut them into 1 cm rounds. Add them to a pan along with the garlic, thyme, stock cube and about a mug full of water (250 ml).

Cover with a lid and bring to the boil then reduce to a simmer and cook for 5-10 minutes or until the water has evaporated and your sprouts are at a consistency you like (I quite like mine over cooked but I know that is not the general consensus - each to their own).

When they are ready stir in the butter and let it melt. Add salt and pepper if needed. Finish off with a small squeeze of lemon juice, if using.

INGREDIENTS

1 lb Brussel Sprouts (or enough
to feed 4 people)
1 large Garlic Clove, crushed
1 tbsp Parsley, chopped
4 tbsp Breadcrumbs
4 tbsp Parmesan Cheese, grated
Splash of Olive Oil
Sprinkle of Salt and Pepper.

Yummy Brussel Sprouts Take 2

Serves 4

I am not sure these will convert the die-hard Brussel haters but I know I enjoy them that is for sure!!

INSTRUCTIONS

Remove any dirty outer layers of the spouts then cut them in half. Blanch in boiling water for about 5 minutes or until they are just nearly cooked. Drain and place them in a casserole dish.

Mix together the breadcrumbs, parmesan, crushed garlic, parsley, salt, pepper and a splash of olive oil. Sprinkle the breadcrumb mixture over the sprouts and bake in an oven (oven at 400°F / 200 °C / Gas Mark 6) for about 15 minutes or until the breadcrumbs have turned a lovely toasty brown.

INGREDIENTS

1 Butternut Squash, peeled
2 Garlic Cloves, thinly sliced
1 Red Chilli, deseeded and sliced
5 fresh Sage Leaves, finely sliced
Pinch of Salt and Pepper
50g Breadcrumbs
Splash of Olive Oil

Roasted Squash and Chilli

Serves 4

You can use less or more chilli depending on your heat preference. Why not try adding a sprinkling of parmesan about 10 minutes before the end of cooking for another flavour combination.

INSTRUCTIONS

Cut the squash into bite sized cubes and place in a roasting tray. Sprinkle over the garlic, chilli, sage, salt and pepper. Add a splash of oil then give it a good mix. Bake in an oven (oven at 400°F / 200 °C / Gas Mark 6) for about 20 minutes then remove from the oven.

Add another small splash of oil to the breadcrumbs and give that a mix then sprinkle over the top of the squash. Return to the oven and cook for another 10 minutes or until tender and golden.

INGREDIENTS

Splash of Olive Oil
1 lb of French Green Beans
2 tsp of each, Garlic Salt, Cumin Seeds, Coriander Seeds, Mustard Seeds
1 tsp Dried Coriander Leaf
Pinch of Dried Chilli Flakes
Pinch of Salt and Pepper

Spicy Green Beans

Serves 4

I found this recipe in a cook book but as so very often I have added in some ingredients and taken some out to make it my own. Serves really well with almost any type of curry but especially a meaty one as it adds a real freshness to the dish.

INSTRUCTIONS

Cut the tops and tails off the green beans if not already done for you.

Cook them in boiling water for approximately 3-5 minutes or until just starting to soften (just tender).

Once par cooked drain and add them back into the pan.

Add in all the other ingredients and fry on a medium heat until they just starting to brown and have softened up a little more while absorbing all the flavours.

4 jacket sized Potatoes (or enough to feed 4 people)
3 tbsp Butter
3 Garlic Cloves, crushed
A pinch of Thyme
Salt and Pepper

200g of Plain Flour
½ tsp of each, Sugar, Salt and Baking Powder
70 ml of Natural Yoghurt
4-5 tbsp of Water
Salted Butter or Garlic Butter for brushing on top once cooked

Garlic Layered Potatoes

Serves 4

This is a similar side dish to dauphinoise potatoes but without the cream. It only uses a few ingredients so a great option for last minute dinner guests. It serves great with any meat or poultry.

INSTRUCTIONS

Peel your potatoes then cut them into thin, even slices. Place the butter, garlic, thyme. salt and pepper in a pan and melt on a gentle heat.   Add the sliced potatoes and give it a good stir to ensure that all the potatoes are covered with the butter. Transfer them to a casserole dish and spread out as evenly as you can.

Cover with foil and bake in the oven (oven at 400°F / 200 °C / Gas Mark 6) for around 30 minutes. Take off the foil and continue to bake until the potatoes have gone soft and are starting to brown. This should take another 30 minutes.

Easy Peasy Naan Bread

Serves 4

I had never made homemade naan bread until a friend of mine promised me it was the easiest thing in the world to make. So I gave it a go and she was right!! It doesn't taste as authentic as when you go for a restaurant curry but it is definitely nicer than shop bought ones. To make it even tastier brush it with garlic butter at the end of cooking.

INSTRUCTIONS

Add the flour, sugar, salt, baking powder and yoghurt to a bowl then gradually add the water and mix until it forms a dough. Add a few drops of oil to your hands then knead the dough mixture for a couple of minutes. Place the dough back in the bowl and leave to rest for about 15 minutes.

When ready divide the mixture into four and roll them out. Place under the grill for about 2 minutes on each side or until cooked and just starting to puff up and go slightly brown. Once ready brush the naan with either salted butter or garlic butter. You could also add chopped chillis if you like it hot!

INGREDIENTS

65g Butter
75g Sugar
1 large Egg
2 large over ripe Bananas
1 tsp Vanilla Extract
85g Plain Flour
1 heaped tsp Baking Powder
3 tbsp Chocolate Chips
2 tbsp Cocoa Powder (optional)

Chocolate Banana Loaf

This is a tried and tested recipe for about the only thing sweet I can cook and cook well (most times). I don't eat a lot of desserts but I do like a nibble of this tasty loaf. Andy and Lauren don't like the banana flavour, even though it is quite mild, but that just means more for us!! The recipe is for a small loaf as normally it is just Adam eating it but you can easily double the ingredients. Note you will have to add extra cooking time if you go for a bigger loaf.

INSTRUCTIONS

Heat Oven to 370°F / 190 °C / Gas Mark 4

Use a 23 x 13 x 7cm Loaf Tin, Buttered and Floured

Melt the butter in a bowl in the microwave. Add the sugar and whisk until it blends together and becomes light and fluffy. Now add the egg and whisk again until it has also blended.

In a separate bowl mash the bananas using a fork. Add the banana mixture to the butter, sugar and egg mixture and stir. Add in the vanilla extract.

Add the flour and baking powder to the mixture and give it a good mix. Finally add your chocolate chips and cocoa powder (if using). Give it a final stir to make sure it is all evenly combined. Pour your mixture into the loaf tin and bake for approximately 35-40 minutes.

When the cooking time is up use a knife or a toothpick to insert into the centre of the loaf. If it comes out clean then it is ready. If not just put it back in the oven for another 5 minutes or until it is ready. Once cooked leave the loaf on a rack to cool before taking out of the tin.

In this recipe I have added cocoa powder to make it really chocolatey as Adam likes it that way but you can leave it out no problem. Try adding different ingredients like nuts (walnuts are a classic) or why not try raisins soaked in a liquor or whisky!! To store the loaf I wrap it in foil and just cut into slices as and when it is needed but I can promise you it doesn't last very long in our house!

INGREDIENTS

2 cups Flour
2 tbsp Sugar
2 tsp Baking Powder
1 tsp Salt
2 cups Milk
3 Eggs
2 tbsp Vegetable Oil

Having the chocolate chips in this recipe you don't actually need to serve anything else with it. But if you are making the waffles without the chocolate chips then maybe drizzle over some maple syrup, honey or even chocolate sauce. Or why not try topping it with fruits like strawberries or blueberries? You could be super indulgent and add a dollop of cream to finish off. The choices are endless.

Choc Chip Waffles

Serves 4

Adam loves waffles and came across this recipe a while back and he has been making it ever since. He vamped it up to "Adam style" by adding chocolate chips. Who doesn't like chocolate he says??

INSTRUCTIONS

Add the flour, sugar, baking powder and salt to a bowl and give it a stir.

Now add in the milk, eggs and vegetable oil and give it a good mix. Don't worry if you have a few lumps. Then add the mixture to your waffle maker and cook until golden brown.

This should take about 3-5 minutes.

Wicked, Weekend, Waffles made in no time – what a sweet treat!!

INGREDIENTS

200g Butter
260g Sugar
3 Eggs
2 tsp Vanilla Extract
125g Plain Flour
3 tbsp Cocoa Powder
200g Chocolate (milk or dark)
Pinch of Salt

Try adding different ingredients like walnuts, cherries or even chilli (it is surprisingly good!!). To serve just eat at room temperature or Adam likes to re-heat his and serve with ice-cream – ooh the indulgence!!

Brownie Heaven

Normally when making brownies both Lauren and Adam use a box mix and to be fair it is quite tasty. But as the recipe is for a cook book I thought taking a photograph of the instructions on the back of the packet wouldn't cut it!! So Adam set about trying recipe after recipe to find the prefect brownie combination and here it is. Adam says no problem him taking one for the team as he had to eat them all up ready to try out the next recipe - hard life Adam!!

INSTRUCTIONS

Heat Oven to 350°F / 180 °C / Gas 4

Use a 25 x 25 cm Square Baking Tin Sprayed with Cooking Oil

Melt the butter and chocolate in a bowl in the microwave. While they are melting whisk together the eggs, sugar and vanilla extract. Whisk until it becomes thick and creamy.

Once ready add it to the melted butter and chocolate and give it a good stir. Now add the flour, cocoa powder and salt and stir again. Pour it into the baking tin and cook for about 25 minutes.

Once cooked leave the tin on a rack to cool before cutting into slices. This recipe should make around 12 brownies.

175g Plain Flour
50g Sugar
1 tbsp Cocoa Powder
150g Butter
50g Chocolate Chips

You could make individual shortbread cookies by cutting the dough with a cookie cutter and placing on a greased baking tray. You could even go very indulgent and coat the cookies with melted chocolate once they are cooled.

Shortbread

This shortbread is really easy to make so it is a great recipe to get the kids in the kitchen and baking. I have said to store these in an airtight container once they are cooled but to be honest they don't last longer than a day in our house so no need to store them for us!

INSTRUCTIONS

Heat Oven to 325°F / 160 °C / Gas 3
Use a 9 inch Circle Baking Tin

Soften the butter slightly by placing in the microwave very briefly for a few seconds or by leaving it out at room temperature for a while before preparing.

When you are ready to start put all the ingredients in a bowl and beat together until it forms a dough. Then knead the dough lightly for a few minutes.

Spray the baking tin with oil then place the dough in the tin and press out evenly to the edges.

Prick the dough all over with a fork and then mark into 8 wedges using a sharp knife.

Bake for 40 minutes until it is firm and golden then remove and leave to cool slightly before cutting into wedges.

Once cool store in an airtight container.

INGREDIENTS

½ pint of Whole Milk
½ tbsp Brown Sugar
¼ tsp Vanilla Extract
75g Chocolate Chips
Pinch Cinnamon Powder (optional)

You could make this a bit more of a grown up hot chocolate by adding a wee tipple. Whisky, Brandy, Cointreau or Kalua would all work a treat. Just add your shot into the pan at the same time as when you add the milk and sugar.

Indulgent Hot Chocolate

Serves 1

This, as the title gives away, is a very indulgent hot chocolate. Because it is so rich Adam only has it as a replacement to his desserts and not in addition too. That might also be because he adds way more than the 75g of chocolate needed while making his hot chocolate (which by the way he thinks I don't know about!!)

INSTRUCTIONS

Put the milk and sugar in a pan and bring to a simmer. Then take off the heat and add the vanilla extract, chocolate and the cinnamon (if using). Stir well until the chocolate melts into the milk.

Leave the pan for about 5 minutes off the heat to let all the flavours mingle together.

When you are ready to enjoy your treat, reheat the hot chocolate gently until it just starts to simmer. It is now ready to serve in a nice big mug.

Why not be super, super indulgent and sprinkle a few marshmallows over the top. Go hard or go home they say??

INGREDIENTS

400g tin of Custard
½ pint of Cream
60g Plain Chocolate plus
extra Chocolate for grating
1 packet Chocolate Chip Cookies
8 fl oz Sherry

You could really 'choc' this up by adding more melted chocolate to the cream and custard mixture. It would make it very, very rich though so only for the faint hearted! And as always foe me, add any extras to any of the layers to make it your own - go own see what concoctions you can create!!

Cookie Trifle

Serves 4-6

This is a different version of the more traditional trifle but it takes less time to make and in my opinion tastes way better. You could switch the type of cookies/biscuits used here as any type of biscuit would work for this recipe.

INSTRUCTIONS

Melt the chocolate in a bowl over warm water or alternatively in the microwave in small intervals so it doesn't over cook. Once melted add in 2 tablespoons of the custard and leave to cool.

Once the chocolate has cooled place the sherry in a bowl and dip the cookies in one by one. Make sure they are fully submerged and count to at least 5 slowly so the cookies can soak up a good amount of sherry but they don't go mushy. Cover each cookie with the chocolate and custard mixture then place into your serving dish. Individual glasses or a see through trifle bowl would work well here but any serving bowl will do. Make 3 layers of cookies.

Whisk the cream until it is thick but not stiff then mix in the remaining custard and pour it over the layered biscuits. Finish off by grating the remaining chocolate over the top to decorate. Place in the fridge for at least 2 hours before serving.

INGREDIENTS

4 Mars Bars, chopped
4 tbsp Milk
4 tbsp Tia Maria
Vanilla Ice Cream (enough
to feed 4)
10 Chocolate Chip Cookies

You can add extra toppings like chopped nuts here or even add slices of banana in the layers if you fancy. You could also switch the alcohol used. The Mars Bars can also be easily changed to the chocolate of your own personal favourite brand. Just make it your own and have fun.

Mars Bar Sundaes

Serves 4

It will take you less time to make this than eat it as it is so simple yet very, very tasty. A great desert go to for a midweek treat when you are busy with other things in your life.

INSTRUCTIONS

To make this desert look pretty use 4 see through glasses (or normal glasses would work just fine).

Add the mars bars, milk and Tia Maria to a pan and cook on a medium heat. Stir continuously until the mixture has all melted into one. Once ready set aside to thicken slightly as it cools.

Crumble the cookies then set aside.

Fill the glasses with layers of ice-cream, crumbled biscuit and the mars bar sauce. Make your top layers the sauce followed by the crumbled biscuit.

Notes

Index

Printed in Great Britain
by Amazon